NEGRITUDE WOMEN

NEGRITUDE WOMEN

T. Denean Sharpley-Whiting

University of Minnesota Press
Minneapolis / London

For Evelyn, with love

Contents

Acknowledgments

In completing this work I had the assistance of several fellowships. I thank the George A. and Eliza Gardner Howard Foundation for their financial support during the year from August 1999 through July 2000. My former department head at Purdue University, Christiane Keck, deserves special mention for nominating me for the Howard Foundation Fellowship. I also thank Michael Pretina and the Camargo Foundation in Cassis, France, for the solitude that led to a wonderfully productive fall 1999 semester. Gianna Celli, the director of Villa Serbelloni, and the Rockefeller Foundation in Bellagio, Italy, provided a month for reflection in the summer of 2000. I was able to complete *Negritude Women* on the lovely grounds of the Villa Serbelloni overlooking Lake Como. And, last but certainly not least, Purdue University provided an early sabbatical (to go along with an early tenure and promotion review) as well as financial assistance to facilitate my research and travels abroad. The assistance I received at the Bibliothèque nationale de France in Paris and the Archives d'outre mer in Aix-en-Provence was absolutely indispensable to my work.

I extend a thank-you to my reviewers; my appendix coeditor and cotranslator, Georges Van Den Abbeele; Robin A. Moir; and the faculty board of the University of Minnesota Press for their enthusiasm and support.

And, as always, my love to Gilman and Haviland.

Introduction
Caliban's Women

Coined in 1936–1937 by the Martinican poet Aimé Césaire during the writing of his now celebrated *Cahier d'un retour au pays natal,* the word *Negritude,* denoting a poetics, a literary, cultural, and intellectual movement, signaled the birth of a Pan-Africanist literature among black Francophone writers, a "New Negro" from the Francophone world. Although the neologism is readily traceable to Césaire, mapping the concept of Negritude as the inauguration of a black humanism, as a "theory of black cultural importance and autonomy,"[1] remains the stuff of a panoply of critical works. In efforts to provide a genealogy of Negritude, many literary historians begin its evolution by simply recovering the earliest writings of Aimé Césaire, Léon Damas, and Léopold Sédar Senghor, who have been credited with the movement's founding. Indeed, according to Georges Ngal, "les deux textes fondateurs du mouvement de la Négritude . . . dessinent les contours de la matrice du mouvement: revendication, affirmation et illustration de l'identité nègre" [the two founding texts of the Negritude movement . . . sketched the contours of the matrix of the movement: the claiming, affirmation, and illustration of Negro identity].[2] These two texts, written by Césaire and Senghor, could be found within the pages of the student journal *L'Étudiant noir.*

In March 1935, a one-issue, eight-page journal sponsored by the Association des étudiants martiniquais en France appeared on the Paris Left Bank scene. Formerly known as *L'Étudiant martiniquais,* the Antillean organ of expression was rebaptized *L'Étudiant noir* in late 1934. Its objective became decidedly Pan-African; that is, the editorial collective attempted to foster dialogue between the ethnically fractured black

1

student body around educational, racial, and cultural issues. The journal was divided into three parts: "Questions corporatives," "Les Idées et les lettres," and "Avez-vous lu ceci?" The articles in the newly christened organ, authored nonetheless primarily by Antilleans, with the exception of one African, represented a new consciousness among black French-speaking students. In a interview with *Jeune Afrique,* Léon Damas, who did not appear in the journal yet insisted that he actively participated in its founding,[3] related: "[B]y virtue of the rampant colonial system, there was ready opposition of the Martinican to the Guadeloupean, to the Guyanese or to the African. People tried to make us believe, for example, that West Indians were superior to Africans. *L'Étudiant noir* saw itself both as a fighting and as a unifying body."[4]

In his "Nègreries: Jeunesse noire et assimilation,"[5] the student Aimé Césaire wrote of the cause of the generation of new black youth, emancipation versus assimilation:

> [A]ssimilation . . . is a dangerous affair. . . . [B]orn of fear and cowardliness, [it] always ends in disdain and hatred, and it carries within it germs of struggle; struggle of same against the same, that is to say, the worst of struggles.
>
> It is because of this that black youth turn their backs on the tribe of the Elders.
>
> The tribe of Elders says, "assimilation," we respond: resurrection! What do Black Youth want?
>
> To Live!
>
> But in order to truly live, we must remain ourselves.
>
> Negro history is a three-episode drama, and we are touching upon the third.
>
> The Negro was first enslaved: "idiots and brutes," they said. Then they turned toward them with a more charitable regard; and it was said: "They are better than previously thought," and attempts were made to make something of them; they were assimilated, they were sent to their masters' schools. "Grown-up children," they were saying, for only a child is perpetually in the school of his masters.
>
> Black youth today want neither servitude nor assimilation, they want emancipation. . . .
>
> Slavery and assimilation resemble one another: they are both forms of passivity.

During these two periods, the Negro has also been unproductive. Emancipation is, to the contrary, action and creation.

Black youth want to act and create. They want to have their poets, their novelists . . . they want to contribute to universal life, to the humanization of humanity.[6]

Césaire's Negritudian moment is here apparent in his decrying West Indian assimilation and advocating the creation of a new self rooted in a rediscovery of the authentic self—the creation of race consciousness.[7] He describes assimilation as madness, "la folie." Assimilation forces the Negro to "tue en lui le Nègre" [kill the Negro within] in his or her quest to become "autre" [other], "assimilé" [assimilated].[8] Not only is accepting a process so deeply invested in the annihilation of the self, "le soi," foolhardy, eliciting laughter from the whites whom one attempts to mimic, but assimilation also goes against "Nature." The assimilated Negro lives inauthentically. It is only through having "faith in the self" [foi en soi], to live authentically one's situation as black, as decreed by nature, that the Negro saves himself from madness ("qu'il se sauve de la folie") (3).

Césaire concludes his first incursion into cultural and identity politics by pronouncing the need for cultural workers who will write of the black experience, its greatness and its misfortunes. Those who act creatively to articulate black particularity, to create a consciousness of blacks' "being-in-the-world," in Heideggerian terms, advance the universal as well as humanize and revolutionize existing notions of humanity wed to black marginality and inferiority.

In contrast to Césaire's impassioned essay, the twenty-nine-year-old Senghor waxed in measured tones of his admiration of the symbiosis of two fundamentally different yet complementary civilizations—black and white, African and European—represented in the person and writings of the Prix Goncourt–winning black French writer René Maran. Using ideas from African ethnologists Leo Frobenius, Maurice Delafosse, Lucien Lévy-Bruhl, and Robert Delavignette, Senghor took up the concepts of a unique Negro soul, irrationalism, intellectual crossbreeding, and intuition to lay the foundations of his "humanisme noir" in "L'Humanisme et nous: René Maran":

It is thus true that we must strip humanism of all that it is not, not in order to destroy "the old version of man" in us, but in order to revive him. Humanism must set about the discovery and knowledge of self, of a black humanism, in our case, that I would willingly define as: a cultural movement that has the black man as its end, Western reason and the Negro soul as its instruments of research; because one must have both reason and intuition.

Man is like a masterpiece. What little we know of his interior life so rich and so complex has been a "drama, a dual between Reason and Imagination, Spirit and Soul, White and Black," in speaking like Aimé Césaire. However, Maran has come to reconcile these dualities, for there is no conflict here. Today he leads a life of active mediation.[9]

Senghor calls for a new humanism that wholly depends on cultural *métissage,* the blending of hotly contested tropes of blackness and whiteness: intuition versus European analytical reason, spirit versus soul. Senghor would later subvert Comte Arthur de Gobineau's valuation "l'emotion est nègre comme la raison est hellène" [emotion is black while reason is Hellenic] to suit his rehabilitation of Africa.[10] Like Césaire, he advocates a return to the self, knowledge of self, and the rediscovery of African civilizations, values, and institutions—however, this return should not discount the gifts of white, Western civilization. This burgeoning theory of complementarities, which would result in the intellectual exchange and renewal of African and European civilizations, would also become the linchpin of Senghor's black humanism, his Negritude, his new Francophone Negro. According to this theory, Europe will benefit from Africa as it has lost touch with "Man," humanity, its humanism of the Enlightenment era; while Africa will benefit from modernization. Africa, Negroes, blacks, with their gifts of emotion, reasoning through participation rather than abstraction, will bring Europe in touch with its thoroughly mechanized self. In contradistinction to Césaire, Senghor maintains that there are vast differences between assimilation, association, and identification. He invokes "une assimilation qui permettre l'association" [an assimilation that allows association], which will lead to "Civilisation de la Universel, une Civilisation de l'Unité par symbiose" [a Civilization of the Universal, a Civilization of Unity by symbiosis] (315–19, 39–69).

Other contributions to *L'Étudiant noir,* such as "Guignol ouolof," by Paulette Nardal, the only woman featured in its pages, and "Mulâtres . . . pour le bien et pour le mal," by Gilbert Gratiant, poet and professor at the Lycée Schoelcher in Fort-de-France, also reflected the pastiche of ideological positions on the question of race, assimilation, and colonialism in the periodical. Nardal's pithy rumination recounts an encounter at a Latin Quarter café with a Senegalese street vendor dressed rather comically in a mix of infantry and hunting wear, which has the effect of presenting him as a livery servant. He is at the café primarily to entertain white patrons. Nardal, self-described as "a black Antillean woman perhaps too westernized," meditates on her and her companion's range of possible responses to this "caricatural Black man"—who represents "all things highly disagreeable to assimilated Blacks who take themselves seriously"—as he approaches their table.[11] With the other café patrons' white eyes fixed upon them, will they "contribute to the amusement of the idle whites?" Will they, "like Antillean mulatresse[s], whose hearts are full of resentment, remove themselves from the presence of this grotesque Black man, this compatriot with no dignity?" Will they "put on prim airs and pretend not to see him?" (4). In the end, Nardal deduces that race transcends class, degrees of Westernization/assimilation, ethnicity, and nationality. "There is, however, between us and him," she concludes, "in lieu of material solidarity, that relating to color" (4). The contributors to the "Ideas and Letters" section of *L'Étudiant noir* in no way shared a consensus, as Nardal seemed to advocate panblackness and Gratiant and Senghor fell squarely on the side of the cultural *métissage* that Césaire expressly critiqued. In fact, the Martinican Gratiant closed his article, the longest in the serial, on this symbiotic note: "And that which I have acquired from white civilization, and that which I would have preserved from the black via Creole, I want to use as the weapons of deliverance for an authentic black civilization of which, however to my regret, I understand so little."[12]

Rather than exemplifying "les deux textes fondateurs du mouvement de la Négritude," particularly given the equally "negritudinal" ideas expressed by Nardal and Gratiant, as well as *L'Étudiant noir*'s obvious continuation of the race ideology laid out in Nardal's earlier review, *La Revue du monde noir*, Césaire's and Senghor's epigrammatic tracts more accurately point to the emergent race consciousness of two writers—one of whom coined the term *Negritude*—who would go on to be celebrated by critics *grâce à* both the neologism and their intellectual and personal association as founders of the Pan-African literary movement in the Francophone world. To be sure, even before 1935 there were a number of other black Francophone novelistic and journalistic precursors that equally treated the themes of colonialism, labor, class, and race. The most notable among those texts were René Maran's 1921 *Batouala: Véritable roman nègre*; Suzanne Lacascade's 1924 *Claire-Solange, âme africaine*; the journals *La Dépêche coloniale* (1922), *Les Continents* (1924–1926), *Le Paria* (1926), *Le Libéré* (1923–1925), *La Voix des nègres* (1926–1927), *La Race nègre* (1927–1986), *La Dépêche africaine* (1928–1932), *La Revue du monde noir* (1931–1932), and *Le Cri des nègres* (1931–1935); and the June 1932 Marxist-surrealist pamphlet *Légitime défense*. Unlike the work of Césaire et al., however, these journalistic endeavors failed to produce a neologism, a concept, or later a literature, which could encapsulate their racial and cultural politics.

So, in September 1931, when Senghor made the acquaintance of Césaire and the Guyanese Léon-Gontran Damas, the three began a collective process of exploring their conflicting identities with respect to race and culture,[13] the "tormenting question," in the prophetic words of Senghor and later Frantz Fanon, of "Who am I?"—that is, their experiences of being black, African, Antillean, and French.[14] For Césaire and Damas, "in meeting Senghor, [they] met Africa."[15] Through Damas and Césaire, Senghor's horizon was opened to the dynamism of the literary and cultural worlds of West Indians and African Americans living in Paris in the 1930s.

Although a general consensus existed among the poets around Negritude's Pan-Africanist philosophical commitment to affirming blacks' being-in-the-world through literary expression, the snapshots provided by *L'Étudiant noir* merely scratch the surface of the varied ways Césaire, Damas, and Senghor experienced and expressed their Negritudes. In a series of interviews with sociologist Lilyan Kesteloot at the 1959 Black Writers and Artists Conference in Rome, sponsored by the journal *Présence africaine,* Césaire responded that he experienced his Negritude as the acknowledgment of "a fact, a revolt, and the acceptance of responsibility for the destiny of [my] race." For Senghor, Negritude represented "black cultural patrimony, that is to say, the spirit of its civilization," whereas Damas regarded it as the explicit "rejection of an assimilation that negated [my] spontaneity and as a defense for [my] condition as Negro and Guyanese."[16] The tones and styles of Damas's 1937 *Pigments* and Césaire's often-analyzed *Cahier* (1939) are periodically anguish-ridden and volatile, critiquing slavery, the colonial system, the utter fallaciousness of the French program of assimilation; suffering from feelings of exile; evoking biting sarcasm; and searching for an identity and culture rooted in blackness, the West Indies, and precolonial Africa.

In *Pigments,* the first volume of poetry published by one of the triumvirate, Damas writes in his characteristic rhythmic style. It is poetry, according to Senghor, that is "unsophisticated . . . direct, brutish, at times brutal but without vulgarity . . . charged with an emotion cloaked by humor:[17]

> Enough failure
> licking
> bootlicking
> an attitude of superassimilation.[18]

Tired of the mimetic situation lived by the colonized and knowing full well, in the presaging words of Frantz Fanon, that "wherever he goes, the Negro remains a Negro"[19] and that assimilation requires a negation of his spontaneity, Damas continues his revolt against the inauthenticity of this existence in "Solde," a poem dedicated to Aimé Césaire:

> I feel ridiculous
> In their shoes
> in their smoking jackets.
> . . . .
> I feel ridiculous
> among them an accomplice
> . . . .
> hands hideously red
> from the blood of their *ci-vi-li-za-tion*[20]

Damas relates that the process of *devenir français* [becoming French] necessitates loss, repression, rejection. With their bloodied hands, the colonized will have committed cultural suicide, will have sold out, in trying to assimilate a bloodthirsty culture, a *"ci-vi-li-za-tion,"* that negates indigenous cultures and peoples as it simultaneously claims to civilize. And the poet laments his loss:

> Give me back my black dolls
> so that I may play with them

> the naïve games of my instincts
>
> . . . .
>
> recover my courage
> my audacity
> Who I was yesterday
> yesterday
> uncomplicated
>
> >   Yesterday[21]

The poet wants to return to the precolonial black world, an era of innocent games where naïveté and spontaneity supposedly reigned before the
physical uprooting of black bodies for capitalist production, before
European cultural and racial domination.

Damas's slow-burning ire reaches a boil in Aimé Césaire's *Cahier:*

> Because we hate you, you and
> your reason, we call upon
> the early dementia, the flaming madness
> of a tenacious cannibalism.[22]

Reason, Absolute Truth, Logic—ideals held as unique to the European
Enlightenment—are denounced by Césaire in favor of the madness, the
illogical, uncivilized, cannibalistic tendencies ascribed to blacks by
Europeans and accepted wholesale by Antillean *évolués.* Césaire rec-
ognizes the Manichaean nature of the colonial world. If the Negro is
but a "jungle savage,"[23] "a corrosive element, the depository of maleficent powers,"[24] then Césaire, as he writes in *Cahier,* "accept[s] . . .
accept[s] . . . totally, without reserve" the lot of his race.[25] His revolt
against Europe and alienated Antilleans consists of this acceptance and
the reversal of an essentialist dialectic that has rendered Africa and its diaspora inferior and France/Europe/whiteness superior.

Unlike Damas's and Césaire's wounds associated with exilic existence—that is, the state of "inhabit[ing] one place," as Michael Seidel
notes in *Exile and the Narrative Imagination,* "and remember[ing] or
project[ing] the reality of another,"[26] in this case, the Antilles and precolonial sub-Saharan Africa—Senghor's ancestral ties to Africa were
solidly traceable, and his cultural memory of Africa remained clearly, if
not romantically, intact. Reflecting his growing up in the rural villages

of Djilor and Joal in Senegal, Senghor's two collections of poetry, *Chants d'ombre* (1945) and *Hosties noires* (1948), represent rather mythical pilgrimages to the ancestral lands of his childhood interjected with anti-colonialist tropes and Marxian rhetoric:

> Lord God, forgive white Europe!
> Yes, it is true, Lord, that for four centuries of enlightenment
> She has thrown her spit and her baying watchdogs on my lands.
> . . . .
>
> Lord, forgive those who turned Askias into guerilla fighters,
> My princes into sergeants, my house servants into "boys,"
> My peasants into wage earners, and my people into a race of
>   working class.
> For You must forget those who exported ten million
> Of my sons in the leprous holds of their ships
> Yes, Lord, forgive France, which hates all occupations
> And yet imposes such strict occupation on me. . . .[27]

Senghor recounts France's crimes against Africa while simultaneously imploring "Lord God" for forgiveness in light of France's hypocrisy. Senghor also makes mention of the German occupation in this "Prayer for Peace," written after World War II. Oppressed, weakened as a European power, and humiliated by the occupation, France nevertheless handed "whole countries" in Africa over to "Big business," which, in shining its lethal "white sun," gradually turned the idyllic Africa of Senghor's boyhood into a wasteland (69–71). France emptied out the continent's resources during the transatlantic slave trade and later conscripted African boys and men into both world wars to fight for its republican ideals—ideals not extended to the colonized. Senghor knew firsthand the impact of France's wars on Africa: he was drafted into the French army in World War II and detained in prison camps for eighteen months; his elder brother was gassed and left disabled while serving France in World War I.

Despite Negritude's cultural currency in the 1930s and 1940s, it has not lacked critics regarding its exotic tendencies and its sociopolitical efficacy from the 1950s onward. In "Orphée noir," the preface to Senghor's *Anthologie de la nouvelle poésie nègre et malgache de langue française* (1948), Jean-Paul Sartre described Negritude, much to the initial chagrin of Senghor[28] and Léon Damas,[29] as an "antiracist racism," a negative stage in the dialectics of history invented to be destroyed in a move toward synthesis, a universal humanism: "The unity which will come eventually, bringing all oppressed people together in the same struggle, must be preceded in the colonies by what I shall call the moment of separation or negativity: this antiracist racism is the only road that will lead to the abolition of racial differences."[30] Negritude was thus not, for Sartre, the answer to "the Negro problem" in France and other parts of the Francophone world, but a necessary step on the "road" toward resolution. Ironically, however, it was Sartre's preface, his repeated use of the word *Negritude* (even as he called the word "ugly" [301]), and his unchallenged position as a French intellectual that would catapult Negritude into mainstream French literary circles and legitimize it as a philosophy of existence. And only Léopold Senghor, ever the diplomatic statesman, who would become president of Senegal and adopt progressively more conciliatory positions with France, later agreed with Sartre's assessment and conceded to Negritude's "racism," comparing it to forms of Nazism and colonialism:

> Our distrust of European values quickly turned into disdain—why hide it—into racism. We thought—and we said—that we Negroes were the salt of the earth, that we were the bearers of an unheard message—and that no other race could offer it but us. Unconsciously, by osmosis and reaction at the same time, we spoke like Hitler and the Colonialists, we advocated the virtues of blood.[31]

In his essays "De la négritude" and "De l'Exotisme," René Ménil, Marxist, philosopher, and cofounder with Aimé Césaire of the Martinican cultural review *Tropiques,* also critiqued Negritude as a form of black exoticism, an "appetitive self-consciousness" unable to free itself from its ideological straitjacket, its becoming other, hence contributing to continuing European imperialism in the Martinican context.[32] Ménil would go one step further by referring to Senghor's New Francophone Negro as a "petty bourgeois, picturesque Negro! . . . a noble savage."[33] Marcien Towa, contrary to the preceding critics, holds fast to Negritude's political efficacy but nonetheless makes a distinction between Césaire's and Senghor's *bon nègre* Negritude. In *Léopold Sédar Senghor: Négritude ou servitude?* Towa writes caustically:

It is undeniably, in part, under the influence of Senghor that Sartre so easily assimilated Negritude to the quest of the "black soul" and to an "anti-racist racism"; besides, it is effectively Senghor who speaks of the "black soul" and who expresses racist views. If, as is unanimously agreed, Césaire is the more powerful and profound Negritude poet, Senghor is then certainly its principal vulgarizer.[34]

It is undeniable that in their zeal, in Césaire's and Damas's early anti-assimilationist stances, in Senghor's cultural *métissage,* and in the three-some's resistance to colonialism's fleecing of the black world, these canonized Negritude writers lapsed into reductive essentialism, an evo-cation of a specifically "black sensibility," "black spirit," "black soul." Yet every movement, concept, and poetics has its place and time in his-tory. To Charles de Gaulle's declaration that "between America and Europe, there is only the ocean and some dust,"[35] to questions regard-ing the existence of culture in the Antilles and civilization in Africa, Negritude, with its affirmation of blackness, vindication of Africa, pro-motion of a culturally engaged literature in the face of French propagan-da, continuing *missions civilisatrices* in Africa, and nauseating paternal-ism, represented in the 1930s and 1940s a radically progressive and self-actualizing alternative.

Negritude flew in the face of Cardinal Jean Verdier's 1939 introduc-tion to the anthology *L'Homme de couleur,* in which French colonial policy is praised as benevolent and humanitarian, indeed humanizing:

> Nothing is more moving than this gesture of the Frenchman taking his black brother by the hand and helping him to realize his ascension. This certainly hierarchized collaboration, but no less real, this fraternal love that bends itself towards the Black to measure his possibilities of think-ing and feeling; this wisely progressive initiation to all sciences and to all arts, the concern of not too brusquely leading the native from his mi-lieu, from his habits, from his traditions, this art of making him evolve, in a word, through the sage development of his personality towards an improved physical, social, and moral well-being, such appears to us France's colonizing mission in the dark continent.[36]

Negritude would throw down an important gauntlet to French colonial-ism, exposing it as a "murderous humanitarianism," in the words of the Paris Surrealist Group,[37] thoroughly self-serving in its "hierarchized collaboration" and self-affirming in its "fraternal love." Damas denounced French assimilationist policy in his 1938 ethnography *Retour de Guyane:* "No. When one will have made six hundred thousand Negroes into as- similated Frenchmen . . . one will not have resuscitated those who die of hunger, one would not have even decently clothed the future assimilat- ed. . . . A little humility, Sirs, colonial representatives!"[38] And Léopold Senghor, in an essay included in Verdier's volume, methodically present- ed "that which the black man brings" to the world, to culture, and to humanity in his essay "Ce que l'homme noir apporte."[39]

Hence, it was not until the 1950s and 1960s that writers began to take Negritude to task, like René Ménil in "De la négritude" and "Une doctrine réactionnaire: La négritude."[40] And although Frantz Fanon rec- ognized that the notion of the "black soul was but a white artifact" in his 1952 publication *Peau noire, masques blancs,* writings by Negritude poets were scattered throughout this same text.[41] Whatever its concep- tual and philosophical shortcomings, in its engagement with issues of race, identity, color, assimilation, alienation, and exile, Negritude, as a race-conscious cultural movement, raised questions that have continuing relevance in contemporary black Francophone African and Caribbean letters and philosophical thought. In the words of Martinicans Jean Bernabé, Patrick Chamoiseau, and Raphaël Confiant, founders of the cultural movement known as Créolité:

> To a totally racist world, self-mutilated by its own colonial surgeries, Aimé Césaire restored mother Africa, matrix Africa, the black civiliza- tion. . . . Negritude imposed itself then as a stubborn will of resistance trying quite plainly to embed our identity in a denied, repudiated, and renounced culture. . . . Césairian Negritude is a baptism, the primal act of our restored dignity. We are forever Césaire's sons.[42]

NEGRITUDE'S *TRACÉES FÉMININES*

As a primarily literary and cultural Pan-Africanist movement emanat- ing out of the experiences of black Francophone intellectuals in 1920s and 1930s Paris, Negritude is generally studied through the works of Césaire, Senghor, and Damas. For their part, the threesome provide a conspicuously masculine genealogy of their critical consciousness. They credit the Haitian anthropologist Antènor Firmin, Jean-Price Mars's Indigenism, Nicolás Guillen's Cuban Pan-Nègrism, and, more frequently, the writers of the Negro Renaissance, specifically Claude McKay, Langston Hughes, James Weldon Johnson, and Sterling Brown, as well as W. E. B. Du Bois's *Souls of Black Folk*; the philosopher Alain Locke's 1925 anthology *The New Negro: An Interpretation*; Carter G. Woodson's *Opportunity,* the popular organ for the National Urban League; and the National Association for the Advancement of Colored People's political vehicle the *Crisis* as primary influences on their consciousness about matters of race, culture, and identity, and hence on their poetical undertakings. As Senghor revealed, "The general meaning of the word *[Negritude]*—the discovery of black values and recognition for the Negro of his situation—was born in the United States of America."[43]

In the black Francophone world, the poets include René Maran as a precursor, because of the incendiary preface to *Batouala: Véritable roman nègre,* in which he wrote:

> After all, if they die of hunger by the thousands, like flies, it is because one is developing their country. Those who do not adapt themselves to civilization disappear.
>
> Civilization, civilization, pride of Europeans, and their charnel house of innocents, Rabindranath Tagore, the Hindu poet, said what you were one day in Tokyo!
>
> You build your kingdom on cadavers. Whatever you want, whatever you do, you wallow in lies. . . . You are the force that takes precedence over right. You are not a torch, but a fire. Whatever you touch you consume it.[44]

As a colonial administrator in French equatorial Africa, Maran witnessed firsthand and recorded in his ethnographic novel the injustices of the French colonial system. The author of the 1947 *Un homme pareil aux autres,* Maran was not, interestingly, a "race man" of the Du Bois ilk, a cultural nationalist, or an anti-French revolutionary. The "véritable roman nègre" did not exalt "black values," and its author was no less critical of Africans than of his administrative colleagues' slackness in carrying out the spirit of the civilizing missions. His solution was not to do away with French colonialism but to reform the abuses within the system. As Maran aficionado Senghor noted, Maran led a life of "active mediation" as a "métropolitain" who happened to be "de couleur" [of color] and above all else considered himself "a man like all others."[45] But *Batouala*'s preface and a number of pages within the work denouncing serious lapses in colonial policy nonetheless qualify the work as an engaged one. Maran paid dearly for his honesty, for he lost his administrative post. The sensation caused by *Batouala*'s winning the Prix Goncourt led to a series of attacks in the press by other "metropolitains de couleur." The reformist journal *La Dépêche coloniale* skewered Maran in its pages: "A work of hatred: *Batouala* or Slander."[46]

At turns scathing and conciliatory in his criticisms, Maran used *les droits de l'homme* as a leitmotiv to call for colonial reform:[47]

> My book is not a polemic. It arrives, by chance, at its hour. The Negro question is of today. . . . Brothers in spirit, the writers of France, . . . I call on you to redress all that the administration designates under the euphemism "weaknesses." . . . The battle will be difficult. . . . Your task is a noble one. To work then, without delay.[48]

Despite Maran's reformist position on colonialism, one that went directly counter to the ideological positions of the three Negritude writers as well as Maran's own "tendency to see racism in the term *[Negritude]* rather than a form of new humanism,"[49] both Damas and Senghor claim him as a Negritude forerunner in "From René Maran to Negritude" and "René Maran, précurseur de la négritude," respectively.[50]

The masculinist genealogy constructed by the founding poets and shored up by literary historians, critics, and Africanist philosophers continues to elide and minimize the presence and contributions of French-speaking black women to Negritude's evolution.[51] Among such neglected proto-Negritude writers is Suzanne Lacascade.[52] In her first and only novel, *Claire-Solange, âme africaine* (1924), Lacascade offers this dedication: "To my African ancestor mothers, to my Creole grandmothers."[53] It is a provocative one for the year in which the work was published. In 1924, there was not another black Antillean writer, male or female, who dared to write such a dedication, who dared to write such a novel. If René Maran's ethnographic *Batouala* earned him simultaneously a literary prize, the scourge of the press and colonial administration, and an exalted place in the genealogy of Negritude because of its ethnographic content and denunciation of the missteps of French colonialism, Lacascade's Africanist and Creole literary endeavor, published only three years after *Batouala*, doomed her to erasure. As novelist Maryse Condé suggests with respect to black Francophone women writers like Lacascade, "[W]henever women speak out, they displease, shock, disturb."[54]

Claire-Solange was certainly not a work of the dime-store interwar variety that was mass-produced and readily dismissed as not literary enough by highbrow critics. Structurally Lacascade pulls out all the novelistic stops; the text has a lyrical quality as it periodically inserts Antillean songs and descriptions of the beguine, a Martinican folk dance, and shifts to an epistolary form and then back to a narrative mode. It was published by the respectable *maison d'éditions* Eugène Figuière, whose authors included Jean Finot, the noted antiracist; Finot was also black clubwoman Mary Church Terrell's intellectual companion in Paris. The author of *Claire-Solange* possessed a literary and musical erudition handily demonstrated through intertextuality. In the novel, composer Robert Schumann's *Carnaval* is infused with Creole rhythms and words. A dialogue on black female subjugation is compared to Andromache's revolt; Charles Baudelaire's idyllic reveries of "la brune enchanteresse," Jacques-Henri Bernardin de Saint-Pierre's Virginie, George Sand's *Indiana,* and Pierre Loti's ethnographic texts are all invoked to expose stereotypical French ways of knowing.

Lacascade's situation as a black Francophone woman writer in the early 1920s, her identification with Africa, her writing in French imbued with Creole expressions, her rich descriptions of Martinican cultural practices, and her denunciations of French racism and anti-Semitism combined to relegate her to the dustbin of black Francophone letters of the era and in years to come. Despite Jean Bernabé's insistence that the Creole literary tradition harks back to the eighteenth century, the Creole language has swung on the race-and-culture pendulum in France and the West Indies as, alternately, a marker of inferiority and a culturally and linguistically viable language in need of preservation and institutionalized dissemination.[55] Léon Damas explored the West Indian preoccupation with speaking the "French of France, French French" in *Pigments,* and Aimé Césaire bristled at the suggestion of writing in any language other than French in a 1940s interview published in the 1978 complete edition of *Tropiques.*[56]

Unlike woman writer Mayotte Capécia, whose troubling racial themes and use of the Creole language in *Je suis Martiniquaise* (1948) would garner her a metropolitan readership and a literary prize while immediately estranging her from the Negritude crowd,[57] Lacascade employed racial awareness and critiques of French racialism that conflicted with establishment politics, literary and otherwise, in the acquiescent colonies and in the *métropole*. Rarely would an Antillean in 1924 have proudly called herself or himself African instead of French. More rarely still would an educated West Indian have published her or his first novel as an act of cultural preservation by an adding an appendix and a vocal recording of Antillean songs in Creole. For Lacascade there is a unique richness that defines Antillean culture, from the "triple baiser à la créole" to the recipes for the "plats créoles" prepared by a Martinican *da*. (*Da* is the Creole word for "nanny" or "nursemaid.") Lacascade's cultural and race politics placed her at odds with the predominantly bourgeois Antillean literati and French metropolitan readers, notwithstanding the novel's patriotism stemming from its World War I backdrop; its tried-and-true interracial love story formula, used by most Antillean women authors of the era; and its reconciliatory denouement of racial and cultural identities. By the conclusion of *Claire-Solange*, Lacascade deftly handles the Senghorian question "Who am I?" as well as anticipates Edouard Glissant's community-oriented rephrasing, "Who are we?" Claire-Solange is culturally Antillean and French and of African, Carib, and European ancestry. She is "Creole," as the novel's dedication admits, like her "grandmothers"—black women "born in the New World."[58] But even more interesting, as the author attempts to "[d]efend and glorify the Black Race!" (a Negritude battle cry) and reclaim the word *nègre*, she also endeavors to reconstruct Caribbean womanhood. Race and gender are inextricably bound. The race will be uplifted through the uplift of black womanhood, in nineteenth-century African American clubwomen's parlance. Lacascade invented a narrative strategy steeped in racial essentialism—another defining and importantly critiqued characteristic of Negritude—as a means to articulate an unbroken relationship between Africa and the diaspora in the French West Indies. It is this use of racial essentialism, specifically with respect to the "essence" of black femaleness—novel for the era yet pervasive in later Franco-Caribbean and African poetry, fiction, and nonfiction—that situates Lacascade, like her contemporary René Maran, as a Negritude literary forerunner and forebear. *Claire-Solange*, with its "African soul," is, like Maran's *Batouala*, a "véritable roman nègre."

NEGRITUDE WOMEN, RACE WOMEN

Perhaps the most glaring omissions in Negritude's evolution have been the "by-the-by" analyses of Paulette Nardal's body of ideas, the complete erasure of Jane Nardal, and the ceding of Suzanne Césaire to the surrealist camp. In effect, if African American male writers of the 1920s radicalized the consciousness of the young and aspiring Francophone black writers; if the race-conscious New Negro of the United States planted the seeds of Negritude in the Francophones' collective imagination, then the three future Negritude poets also undeniably received inspiration from Mlles Jane and Paulette Nardal.[59] In a letter written in February 1960, Senghor revealed: "We were in contact with these black Americans during the years 1929–34, through Mademoiselle Paulette Nardal, who, with Dr. Sajous, a Haitian, had founded *La Revue du monde noir.* Mademoiselle Nardal kept a literary salon, where African Negroes, West Indians, and American Negroes used to get together."[60] In correspondence also dated in the year 1960 and sent to Senghor's biographer Jacques Louis Hymans, Paulette Nardal "complained bitterly" of the erasure of her and Jane Nardal's roles in the promulgation of the ideas that would later become the hallmarks of Césaire, Damas, and Senghor. The trio "took up the ideas tossed out by us and expressed them with flash and brio." Essentially, Nardal wrote, "we were but women, real pioneers—let's say that we blazed the trail for them."[61] Having neither a Robert Desnos, the foreword writer for Damas's *Pigments;* a Jean-Paul Sartre; nor an André Breton to attest to their genius and Negritude credentials, the Nardal sisters, particularly Paulette, have been characterized, in the few works that do mention them, as movement midwives rather than architects.[62]

The *soeurs* Nardal, with their Sunday literary salon and review, did more than provide a cultured place (their apartment) and literary space *(La Revue du monde noir)* for the intellectual coming-of-age of Césaire, Damas, and Senghor. Jane Nardal, who published poetry under the pseudonym "Yadhé," invoked Africa in her poems on the Antilles before it became fashionable.[63] Her essay on black humanism, "Pour un humanisme noir," which was scheduled to be published but never appeared in the bilingual *La Revue du monde noir,*[64] served as a model for Senghor's first essay on humanism and René Maran, published in *L'Étudiant noir.*[65] Her essay "Pantins exotiques," which appeared in the October 1928 issue of the newspaper *La Dépêche africaine,* provides a critique of representations of the Negro in the work of best-selling author Paul Morand. Nardal explicitly assails the exoticism of the French colonial literary tradition, implicating equally American literature, specifically

Carl Van Vechten. But more fascinating, Jane Nardal, who has also been overshadowed by the (albeit scant) attention paid to her bilingual older sister Paulette, wrote in February 1928 a defining essay on Pan-Africanism in the Francophone context, titled "Internationalisme noir." In the essay, Jane Nardal discussed the evolving "race spirit" among "après-guerre" Negroes. She also created the neologism "Afro-Latin" to describe the "double consciousness" experienced by the Francophone Negro. It would appear that Césaire, Senghor, and even Paulette Nardal pilfered from the war chest of race theorizing and global consciousness contained within "Internationalisme noir," as it provided a history of the development of the Negro in the Francophone world and encouraged the creation of literature and arts to reflect this race consciousness.

For her part, Paulette Nardal penned a series of essays and a short story during the interwar period in Paris before returning to Martinique to write literature for the colonial administration promoting tourism in the Lesser Antilles and to found a religious, woman-centered serial, *La Femme dans la cité*. In 1929, Nardal wrote two literary pieces, "Actions de grâces" and "En exil." The first essay, written in May 1929, is an autobiographical reminiscence on the Antilles inspired by the arrival of summer in France.[66] In December, Nardal wrote her first short story, "En exil," which explored the themes of exile, alienation, gender, and race.[67] As an intellectual émigré in Paris, Nardal presents a moving tableau of an older Antillean female domestic worker, Elisa, experiencing feelings of displacement, hostility, and cultural and racial alienation in the metropolis, the very feelings that Nardal would later proclaim led to the awakening of race consciousness among black Antillean students in an essay in *La Revue du monde noir*.

In the sixth and final issue of *La Revue du monde noir*, Paulette Nardal published "L'Éveil de la conscience de race chez les étudiants noirs," a comparative cultural, literary, and quasi-political history of African American and Franco-Caribbean letters. Nardal underscored the fact that, unlike the literature of the New Negro in America, Antillean literature had been imitative of French metropolitan themes and resistant to exploring "racial themes." The well-read Nardal, influenced by the New Negro movement and Garveyism, urged her West Indian compatriots to begin researching and writing about the lived experiences of black Antilleans. Nardal's piece clearly articulated what would become defining characteristics of Negritude thought, namely Pan-Africanism, the affirmation of black peoples and their cultural productions, and the rehabilitation of Africa.[68]

Although not totally written out of Negritude history, Suzanne Roussy-Césaire's intellectual legacy has suffered the fate of many talented women married to prominent men—marginalization. As Maryse Condé writes in her article "Unheard Voice: Suzanne Césaire and the Construct of a Caribbean Identity":

> Suzanne Césaire is at the same time a myth and an enigma. We know very little about her. . . . André Breton, the Surrealist poet, praised her beauty, and in the preface to *Return to My Native Land* by Aimé Césaire he writes: "Suzanne Césaire, belle comme la flame du punch" [Suzanne Césaire, as lovely as the fire of rum punch]. Michel Leiris, the French anthropologist who spent several years in Martinique, complained of her aggressiveness in putting forward Communist-oriented ideas and did not believe that it went well with her duties as the mother of five children. More recently, in his critical work *Aimé Césaire: Un homme à la recherché d'une patrie,* Zairean Georges Ngal dismissed her with the stroke of a pen and declared that all her ideas were taken from her illustrious husband.[69]

Domestic duties, fiercely independent critical thinking, ethereal beauty, and a famous husband all combined to eclipse Suzanne Césaire's literary career. Her philosophical acumen, demonstrated in essays such as "Le Grand camouflage," "Misère d'une poèsie," and "Malaise d'une civilisation," has been dwarfed in critical literature on Negritude by preoccupations with Aimé Césaire's artistry. As Michael Richardson, the editor of *Refusal of the Shadow,* a volume on surrealism and the Caribbean, notes in contrast to the typical dismissals of Suzanne Césaire's individual intellectual merits put forth by critics such as Georges Ngal: "For [Aimé] Césaire [surrealism] was essentially a poetic tool, a means to use language, and a moral sensibility. . . . For . . . Suzanne Césaire, on the other hand, surrealism was more of a critical tool, a means of reflection that would provide [her] with a critical foundation from which to explore [her] own cultural context."[70]

Distressed by what she perceived as a "cultural void" in Martinique, in 1941 Suzanne Césaire, Aimé Césaire, and René Ménil cofounded the review *Tropiques.* Their encounter with the ubiquitous father of French surrealism, André Breton, in Martinique in 1941 added a different dimension to Negritude thought. Suzanne Césaire wrote in 1943: "Surrealism, the tightrope of our hope."[71] In a series of seven essays written between 1941 and 1945, she invariably used a surrealist-inflected Negritude and Leo Frobenius's ethnology to theorize about the transformational power of words and to challenge the Martinican literary bourgeoisie—who would eventually call for the review's suppression—to write an authentic literature, a literature engaged with the genius of indigenous Martinican culture.

Negritude Women is, thus, an essentially female-centered literary history whose goal is to provide a corrective to male-centered analyses of Negritude. This critical feminine genealogy will trace the history of the idea of Negritude and its evolution through the essays of black Francophone women intellectuals, namely Jane Nardal, Paulette Nardal, and Suzanne Césaire. The selection of these three women intellectuals has as much to do with the philosophical and theoretical dimensions of their bodies of work, which directly reflect the race and cultural ideology of Negritude in its various evolutionary phases, as with their direct involvement with and influence on those "founding" writers of canonical Negritude literature. The present volume is not especially interested in the fictional and/or poetic representations produced by women writers of the 1930–1950 era that may or may not reflect Negritude ideology, but rather with nonfictional essays that did in fact present the schema, the architecture, for a new literature and humanism in the black Francophone world. The seventeen-year period covered by the work, from 1928 to 1945, marks the emergence and the exit of these three women writers on the Negritude scene. By 1948, Sartre had picked up on the word *Negritude* and heralded its emergence as a new literary and philosophical movement in highly masculinized language on the French intellectual landscape, even though its philosophical praxis had been ongoing and its theoretical precepts woman-generated. Negritude may have been new to Sartre, but not to the *soeurs* Nardal and Suzanne Césaire.

That all three women are from Martinique, rather than other parts of the French empire, points to French colonial idiosyncrasies and not to any deliberate authorial choices.[72] Martinique held the particularly interesting role of crown jewel of the French Antilles. Before its destruction in the 1902 eruption of the volcano Mount Pelée, St. Pierre, the former capital of Martinique, was known as the "Little Paris" of the

Caribbean. In South America, Guyana was reduced to a penal colony, and the French had only begun, in comparison to the "vieilles colonies," their civilizing missions in Africa. As literary critic Clarisse Zimra concludes in her 1984 article "Négritude in the Feminine Mode: The Case of Martinique and Guadeloupe," which explores literature written primarily by post-1945 women writers, "Martinique was always the more favored island, with a higher proportion of Whites, better economic development, [and] a more favorable position on the power ladder of colonialism."[73]

The reader will also notice that, unlike other literary histories of Negritude, this one does not begin in 1932 with *Légitime défense,* and with good reason. In this gendered remapping of the movement's origins, the present study begins four years earlier with *La Dépêche africaine,* fast-forwards to 1931–1932 with *La Revue du monde noir,* and then shifts to *Tropiques* in 1941–1945. This introduction has importantly included an overview of the fabled 1935 *L'Étudiant noir,* which also featured Paulette Nardal and Aimé Césaire and Senghor. *Légitime défense,* as will be rearticulated in chapter 5, was primarily a Marxist-surrealist endeavor; it was not a journal of Negritude. For his part, René Ménil, a contributor, has noted that the only conceptual idea this organ, also founded by Martinican students, shared with Negritude was an emphasis on a black sensibility.[74] For their part, Césaire and Senghor have maintained that *Légitime*'s writers produced no literature that was distinguishable from their surrealist masters. More importantly, any vaguely race-conscious-related criticisms issued in the pamphlet's twenty-two pages, by Ménil and Étienne Léro in particular, came after and were importantly influenced by both Nardals' essays in *La Dépêche africaine* and *La Revue du monde noir.*

This work proceeds, then, chronologically and thematically, comprising five chapters and an edited appendix of translations of selected writings by both Nardals and Suzanne Césaire. In taking up readings of these essays, *Negritude Women* defers to the masculinist language of the time used by the Nardals and Césaire when referring to "the poet" and "the Antillean writer." Clearly exhibiting gender consciousness, these Martinican women were nevertheless products of a French educational system in which "L'homme" and "il" in the *déclaration des droits de l'homme* were naturalized as neutral and gender-inclusive. Trying to ascertain whether these women were feminists in the American sense of the word is necessarily fraught with cultural complications, for *féministe* in the France and Martinique of 1920–1950, and even today, does not readily translate with the same "engaged" nuances. A word about the usage of the derogatory term *mulatto* in the volume is also important. So long as the spirit of the writer's meaning is not compromised, the commonly used *mulatto* will be substituted with the terms *métis* or *mixed race*. The word *métis* also comes with caveats, as it covers a range of multiracial categories in France.

Chapter 1, "Race Signs of the Interwar Times: Pan-Noirisme and *La Dépêche Africaine*," provides a historical overview of the interwar period in France and the nascent international black movements, organizations, and newspapers in Paris. The interactions between black Francophone and Anglophone intellectuals such as W. E. B. Du Bois, Addie Hunton, Kathyrn Johnson, Mercer Cook, René Maran, and Blaise Diagne, and the various ideologies on race and colonialism, from Du Boisian Pan-Africanism to Garveyism and from militant colonial reformism to assimilationism, are also explored. The colonial-reformist newspaper *La Dépêche africaine* (1928–1932) is examined in depth, as it was the first vehicle for the race-conscious cultural and social expressions of Jane Nardal. The newspaper also clearly had Garveyist ties and Pan-Africanist leanings.

"Jane Nardal: A New Race Spirit and the Francophone New Negro," chapter 2, takes up a reading of Jane Nardal's 1928 essays "Pantins exotiques," which deftly levels a challenge to modernism, and "Internationalisme noir," which prophesies the formation of a new race spirit in Lockean terms and the formation of a global diasporic community. Chapter 3, "Les Soeurs Nardal and the Clamart Salon: Content and Context of *La Revue du monde noir*, 1931–1932," probes the first multiracial, gender-inclusive salon in Paris set up by black Francophone women, the Clamart salon, and the Parisian climate that led to its creation. Exchanges between writers, intellectuals, and artists like Nancy Cunard and the *soeurs* Nardal, and events literary and political, such as the 1931 Colonial Exposition at the Bois de Vincennes in Paris, that influenced discussions on race and identity among black Francophone intellectuals in the 1920s and 1930s and that culminated in the founding of *La Revue* are addressed. While providing the reader with a snapshot of the *La Revue du monde noir*'s cultural and sociological contents and its colonial-reformist ideological orientation, chapter 3 also examines the cultural review's stated aims—to globalize black consciousness, to defend blacks' collective interests, and to "glorify their race"—as thematic preludes to Césaire's coining of the word *Négritude.*

Chapter 4, "Paulette Nardal: Antillean Literature and Race Consciousness," examines Nardal's last and only politically charged contribution to what would be *La Revue*'s final issue, in 1932. Nardal's deft narration of "race consciousness" among Antilleans in Paris and her provocative call for more studies on black identity in the French context prompted students such as Césaire, Senghor, and Damas to change their courses of study, and the Ministry of the Colonies to withdraw financial support from the review.

Chapter 5, "Suzanne Césaire: *Tropiques,* Negritude, Surrealism, 1941–1945," provides a historical framework for examining the social, cultural, and political issues leading up to the founding of *Tropiques* and an overview of the articles and poetry within the magazine's pages. The chapter analyzes Suzanne Césaire's appropriation of surrealism and Leo Frobenius's ethnology as a vehicle for Negritude cultural politics in the essays "Malaise d'une civilisation" and "Le Grand camouflage." The volume closes with an edited and annotated appendix of translated writings by Jane and Paulette Nardal and Suzanne Césaire that are examined throughout *Negritude Women,* as well as the letters exchanged between the editors of *Tropiques* and Nazi-collaborating Vichy officials in 1943.

Like Shakespeare's Caliban from *The Tempest,* whose name is a near anagram of *cannibal,* "profit[ing] on" Prospero's language to "curse" upon Prospero a "red plague" (1.2.366–67), these Negritude women cannibalized the philosophical and ethnological tools of French culture to infuse in its interstices a new consciousness about race. As Caliban's women—women of that "abhorred slave" race (1.2.355)—they represent a glaring absence in terms of sexual and reproductive desire, given that Caliban pursues Miranda to "peopl' else / This isle with Calibans" (1.2.353–54).[75] Their voices hardly register in the historico-literary record relating to the production of knowledge on the race. In the words of the Guadeloupean woman writer Maryse Condé, "It is an accepted fact that French Caribbean literature was born with Negritude."[76] But what is not such a widely accepted or acknowledged fact is that women writers and thinkers were at the movement's historical and philosophical centers and, often, at the vanguard. *Negritude Women,* then, focuses on the ways in which writings by Jane Nardal, Paulette Nardal, and Suzanne Césaire are critical to providing a definitive, gender-inclusive history of Negritude as the moment when a new literature and philosophy of black humanism among black Francophone intellectuals was born.

1. Race Signs of the Interwar Times: Pan-Noirisme and *La Dépêche Africaine*

It is a peculiar sensation, this double consciousness, this sense of always looking at one's self through the eyes of others, of measuring one's soul by the tape of a world that looks on in amused contempt and pity. One ever feels his two-ness—an American, a Negro; two souls, two thoughts, two unreconciled strivings; two warring ideals in one dark body, whose dogged strength alone keeps it from being torn asunder.
—W. E. B. Du Bois, *The Souls of Black Folk*

In February 1928, the journal of the Comité de défense des intérêts de la race noire (CDIRN), *La Dépêche africaine,* was published in Paris under the editorial direction of the Guadeloupean Maurice Satineau, secretary of the *comité,* with a prestigious multiracial board of collaborators, including lawyers; *femmes de lettres* such as Carly Broussard and Marcelle Besson; award-winning writers like René Maran; and Charles Bellan, former president of French Indochina. The newspaper's motto—"Défendre nos colonies, c'est fortifier la France" [To defend our colonies, is to fortify France]—sums up the interesting patchwork of militant colonial reformism, assimilationism, and cultural Pan-Africanism found in its monthly columns. Serving as a means of correspondence "between Negroes of Africa, Madagascar, the Antilles, and America," *La Dépêche africaine* maintained, in the assimilationist and colonial reformist fashion of the era, that "the methods of colonization by civilized nations are far from perfect; but colonization itself is a humane and necessary project."[1] As the spiritual inheritor of René Maran and Kojo Tovalou's defunct bimonthly, *Les Continents, La Dépêche africaine* consistently evoked the ideas of France 1789 and Schoelcherism, that is, the liberal principles of Victor Schoelcher, a French administrator responsible for the abolition of slavery in the colonies. In this *après-guerre* France, where unemployment emerged unchecked alongside xenophobia, racism, and paternalism; where primitivism—the realm of the Negro—became the rage in Paris in attempts to forget a war-ravaged and morally bankrupt Europe, and exotic literature amply filled in the spaces in between, black French-speaking intellectuals wanted to revivify France as a paragon of liberty, fraternity, and equality, a civilizing and civil nation.

Fissures around class and ethnicity had previously confounded efforts toward multiethnic organizing among the primarily bourgeois Antillean and working-class African populations in the metropolis. Many Antilleans, however, came to realize that the racist capriciousness and inequities experienced by Africans imperiled them as well. As Malagasy and Senegalese soldiers in World War I were unevenly compensated and promises of citizenship used as a recruitment method went largely unfulfilled, *bien-aisé* assimilated Antilleans were subjected to the "tutoyer" by working-class whites.[2] Consequently, multiethnic newspapers and organizations like the Antillean native Maran and Dahomean Kojo Tovalou's *Les Continents,* Guadeloupean Oruno Lara and Malagasy Samuel Stéfany's *Le Monde colonial,* and the Ligue des droits de l'homme and the Ligue universelle de défense de la race noire sprang up in Paris.

The first European World War also brought French-speaking blacks into contact with African Americans, further globalizing their understanding of racial inequality and oppression.[3] W. E. B. Du Bois, Harvard graduate, professor, author of the 1903 book *The Souls of Black Folk,* and editor of the National Association for the Advancement of Colored People's organ the *Crisis,* organized the first Pan-African Congress in Paris from February 19 to 21, 1919, with the help of elite Francophones of color Blaise Diagne and Gratien Candace. Du Bois, with his theories on the "talented tenth," on "what the Negro brings to America," on the uneasy symbiosis of blackness and Americanness, and on the cultural histories of Africa and its diaspora,[4] found a receptive audience among these Francophone elites, some of whom were attempting to reconcile France's conceptual humanism with its practices to create, oddly enough, a new colonial humanism.

The Senegalese Blaise Diagne, who would later become Léopold Senghor's political mentor, was a deputy in the French Parliament and the trusted adviser to President Georges Clemenceau. From his petit bourgeois beginnings in Île de Gorée, Senegal, and education in Aix-en-Provence, France, Diagne rose through the ranks of the colonial administration. Developing a taste for politics, he ran for a seat in the French Chamber of Deputies in the National Assembly. Winning because of various factions in the opposing party and the suggestion by one French candidate that "it was impossible to appeal intelligently to illiterate African voters," Diagne entered the National Assembly in Paris as its first black African deputy at the dawn of World War I, in July 1914.[5] Like Diagne, who helped recruit—or, as some like René Maran would argue, duped—Senegalese soldiers to fight for France with the promise of French citizenship, the patriotic Du Bois encouraged black Americans to enlist in the war effort. Du Bois hoped that black participation in the fight for freedom abroad would translate into better treatment for African Americans at home. Both men were mistaken in their calculations of white American and French gratitude and benevolence, and the credibility and currency of both were dealt serious blows in the camps of their black American and African constituents. Nevertheless, Du Bois was a great admirer of the principles of Jacobin France. Surmising that France was free of the accursed veil, of the "hateful, murderous, dirty *Thing* which in America we call 'Nigger-hatred,'" Du Bois "chose to deceive himself into believing [France] discriminated on the basis of culture rather than color."[6] Thus, his anticolonialist and anti-imperialist tendencies were tempered by an enduring respect for France. In fact, when contrasting Du Bois's anti-imperialist and antiracist politics with those of Marcus Garvey, French government agents referred to Du Bois as "moderate."[7] And they were certainly right in their assessment, for Du Bois wept joyous tears and wrote the article "Vive la France" (March 1919), which recounted the ceremony organized by the Ligue colonial at the Place Trocadero to honor soldiers who had fought in France's various colonial wars. As Du Bois biographer David Levering Lewis suggests,

> Had Marcus Garvey witnessed the spectacle in the Trocadero, he would hardly have been elated to see blacks honored by their colonial masters for service that had prolonged their own subordination and exploitation. That Du Bois, author of "The African Roots of the War" and impresario of Pan-Africanism, saw no irony, paradox, and certainly no pathos . . . was a measure of the eccentric Eurocentrism and radicalism-from-above that still resided in the marrow of the author of *The Souls of Black Folk*.[8]

Du Bois's Pan-Africanism, then, did not initially prove a serious threat to the French colonial policy that many *métropolitains de couleur,* particularly the Senegalese Blaise Diagne, held as almost sacrosanct for the advancement of the "races retardataires" [backward races] of Africa.[9]

It was, importantly, the Great War that initially brought Du Bois to France. The valiant efforts of the black divisions of the American Expeditionary Forces in France, as well as the discrimination to which they were daily subjected by their white American counterparts, required investigation and recording. Addie Hunton and Kathryn Johnson certainly contributed to this endeavor with their book *Two Colored Women with the American Expeditionary Forces* (1920). Both women served as Young Men's Christian Association (YMCA) volunteers for the black troops in France. Their work provides insight into the morale of the soldiers at various battlefronts such as Verdun, the interactions between the French and the black soldiers, and the beginning of the Jazz Age in France. Hunton, who also attended the first Pan-African Congress in Paris, closes *Two Colored Women* with an "afterthought" that aptly characterizes the esteem in which black Americans—soldiers on the battlefront, intellectuals like Du Bois, and spectators of the war on the American home front—held France:

> Approximately 150,000 soldiers, officers and men went to France to represent the colored race in America. Many of them were brigaded with the French, while other thousands had a contact and association with this people which resulted in bringing for the entire number a broader view of life; they caught the vision of a freedom that gave them new hope and new inspiration.
>
> And while they traveled, they learned that there is a fair-skinned people in the world who believe in the equality of the races, and who practice what they believe.
>
> In addition to this they had an opportunity of making a record for themselves that will be in no [way] hidden from the generations of the future; a proud record of which the Frenchman took note, and for which he will give them due credit in the true history of the Great World War.[10]

France alone, as a great number of Anglophone and Francophone blacks of the era contended, thoroughly believed and practiced racial equality. Hunton's prediction regarding the French preservation for future generations of the legacy of black Americans' participation in "the Great War World" was sadly accurate. As America erased black men and women's contributions to the war effort in its aftermath, France's cultural and historical memory and gratitude were unfailing.[11] Hunton and Johnson were not the only blacks who felt compelled to leave an African American historical record on the war. W. E. B. Du Bois and the NAACP also weighed in, putting Du Bois's journalistic skills to use in recording the history of the Negro soldiers in World War I.

As an aftereffect of the war, a peace conference at Versailles was also held. Du Bois was charged by the NAACP to serve as a representative at the conference. Besides the never-completed three-volume history of the soldiers' efforts tentatively titled "The Wounded World," Du Bois's presence in France allowed him to undertake another project for which he had received approval from the NAACP board in October 1918, which he deemed of equal importance to the "Negro" race. In "Negro at Paris," Du Bois wrote rather optimistically:

> I went to Paris because to-day the destinies of mankind center there. Make no mistake as to this my dear readers.
>
> In fine, not a single great serious movement or idea in Government, Politics, Philanthropy or Industry in the civilized world has omitted to send and keep in Paris its Eyes, Ears and Fingers! And yet some Negroes actually asked why I went to help represent the Negro world in Africa and America and the Islands of the sea. What could a Pan-African Congress do?
>
> We got, in fact, the ear of the civilized world. . . . As it was, we organized the Pan-African Congress as a permanent body, with Mr. Diagne as president and myself as secretary, and we plan an international quarterly, *Black Review,* to be issued in English, French, and possibly Spanish and Portuguese.
>
> The world-fight for black rights is on![12]

The congress brought together fifty-eight delegates from sixteen countries, including various countries in Africa and the Antilles, the United States, and Great Britain, at the Grand Hotel at le boulevard des Capucines.[13] Two significant motions were eventually passed. The first was very much in keeping with the French policy on the *évolué* and the elitist persuasion of the congress; that is, only "evolved" or cultured and civilized persons of African descent would be accorded citizenship rights. The right to request that various rights of citizenship be conferred was reserved for the elites. The second motion involved addressing the League of Nations regarding rights violations of "civilized" citizens of Negro descent by sovereign states. The political maneuverings of congress president Blaise Diagne combined with the secretary Du Bois's political idealism toward France to safeguard French colonial policy in Africa. Unlike other European imperialist countries, France escaped wholesale condemnation at future congresses. As André Maginot, a high-ranking French colonial official, later noted approvingly of the congress's position on France: "The Pan-African Congresses held at London in August, and at Paris in September noted that France alone practices racial equality, and admits black representatives in Parliament. They called our colonial undertaking one of 'a splendid beginning.'"[14] If the first congress revealed certain experiential commonalities between blacks throughout the Anglophone and Francophone worlds, the outcome of the second congress, in August and September 1921, resulted in the founding in France of a Pan-African Association. Its goal was "to study and undertake all that may contribute to the betterment of the lot of the black race on all points of the globe."[15] The association's officers hailed from the Francophone West Indies and the United States. Gratien Candace served as president, and Rayford Logan, an American soldier, served as secretary. For *les français noirs,* "betterment" ostensibly translated into colonial reforms that would facilitate assimilation into Frenchness.

Repeatedly calling attention to racial and cultural differences went expressly counter to the French universalism that nurtured these African *évolués* and *métropolitains de couleur.* Lynching and other forms of racial terrorism, legalized segregation, and the denial of citizenship rights to the obviously "evolved" blacks in the United States, viewed by the French populace in general as inhumane and barbarous practices, would never have taken place in the *mère-patrie,* at least in the hearts and minds of these French black intellectuals. French racism could be generally characterized as paternalistic, whereas American racism seesawed between stamping out the very existence of African Americans (via lynching) and reducing them to social outcasts dispossessed of human and civil rights. As René Maran wrote in the article "La France et ses nègres": "The Negro in France is protected, cherished, and by and by treated equally. . . . [C]olonial France is simply in fundamental and constant opposition with France proper."[16] As in his preface to *Batouala,* Maran points to the conduct of French colonial administrators as the proverbial chink in France's egalitarian armor. The idealist Maran insisted that the species of Frenchmen in French Equatorial Africa were wholly different from those in France. As the colonies had been structured to be governed by their own elected political officials, Maran and his breed of French black intellectuals were naive with regard to the complicity of the *métropole* as the central organizing body in their administering. The cleavage between American and Francophone blacks' experiences of race and racism bore itself out even more importantly with Blaise Diagne's progressively coming to regard W. E. B. Du Bois's politics as "dangerously internationalist," hence a threat to French colonial interests.[17] Under both Diagne's and Gratien Candace's conservative auspices, the multilingual review never came into fruition, and the Pan-African Association of France stalled. Candace eventually resigned as president in February 11, 1923, and the number of black Americans in the association dwindled.[18]

Moreover, a formidable grassroots movement for self-determination and "Africa for the Africans," led by Marcus Garvey, sprang forth to siphon off a number of the Anglophone West Indian contingent at the second Pan-African Congress. Garvey's United Negro Improvement Association (UNIA), begun in the United States, was vigorously denounced at the second congress as "poorly conceived," having "demagogic leadership" and "intemperate propaganda."[19] However, in the spirit of global black solidarity, the editors of *Les Continents,* René Maran and Kojo Tovalou, published in their cultural section titled "La Case de l'oncle Tom" articles by Alain Locke, poetry by Langston Hughes, discussions of African American music, and fiery editorials from the UNIA's *Negro World.* Notwithstanding these editorial inclusions, before six hundred people at a gathering at the Gaité-Rochechouart Theatre, Maran reproached Garvey for exempting France from his critiques of colonialism during an October 1928 visit to Paris. Garvey, speaking in English and being translated by a Madame Coblence, "thank[ed] the French" [remercie les Français] in the name of his Assembly of the Negro World for "being so welcoming to blacks in the Metropole unlike in America and England." Maran interjected and corrected Garvey by stating that "[colonial] France acts no differently with Negroes than the others: it is only a question of nuance. French colonization may be less arduous than Anglo-Saxon colonization, but it is nonetheless arduous."[20]

And although he appreciated Garvey's racial rhetoric in the context of American racism, as well as his calls for an independent African state, Kojo Tovalou insisted that the "sionisme noir" [black Zionism] of the UNIA was not appropriate in France. Tovalou, a cofounder of the Ligue universelle de défense de la race noire, was all too familiar with, and unsympathetic to, the American brand of racial politics. He had been pummeled with fists and feet by a group of American tourists in 1923 at a bar in Montmartre and then thrown out by the French proprietor at the request of the Americans, who did not welcome his black presence in the bar.[21] In a revealingly titled address, "Paris coeur de la race noire," given in 1924 before Garveyites at Liberty Hall in New York City, Tovalou concluded:

> Your association, Mr. President Garvey, is the Zionism of the Black Race. It has the advantage in its radicalism of stating clearly the problems, of mapping out the . . . route to our refuge. . . . France is the only country that does not have race prejudice, but struggles for its disappearance. . . . In this country [France], like all countries of Latin origin, one is more receptive to the cults of idealism and humanity. Anglo-Saxon imperialism . . . has not yet atrophied all emotional faculties.[22]

With great aplomb, Tovalou resuscitated the myth of France as tolerant and enlightened with respect to race. Despite inequities in colonial Africa and the West Indies, exposed by Maran in *Batouala* and later by Damas and Césaire in *Retour de Guyane* and *Cahier d'un retour au pays natal*, France proper, when contrasted with Anglo-Saxon antiblack racism, emerged in writings by colonial reformist and assimilationist black Francophone thinkers of the era as more humane and, in both principle and practice, dedicated to egalitarianism. Although neither of the antiracist agendas of the UNIA and the Pan-African Congress were accepted in toto by French black intellectuals in Paris, both movements propagated the seeds of global consciousness, an awareness of the genius of the black race and of a cultural Pan-Africanism that would occupy the pages of journals like *Les Continents* and *La Dépêche africaine*.

With its global readership, *La Dépêche africaine* was quite popular during its four-year publication run.[23] In the November 15, 1928, issue, under the rubric "Une bonne nouvelle" [A bit of good news], the monthly announced that by January 1929 it would become a semimonthly newspaper, appearing on the first and the fifteenth of each month: "The increasingly favorable reception that the colonial and metropolitan public reserves for our organ obliges us to augment our frequency."[24] According to a report filed by the police prefecture with the Ministry of Colonies in November 1928, *La Dépêche africaine* had nearly ten thousand copies in circulation.[25] Yet in January 1929, the newspaper apologized to its readers, explaining that it would "momentarily be unable to appear two times per month as previously announced, due to administrative reorganization."[26] By May 1929, the journal's management settled on publication on the thirtieth of every month.[27] But *La Dépêche africaine* continued to publish inconsistently, on the first, fifteenth, or thirtieth of any given month. Such inconsistency would later be revealed in reconnaissance reports as financially tied. According to a report on the activities of the journal filed by government officials on May 30, 1930, the editors had been scrambling to come up with funds ("Les dirigeants de *La Dépêche africaine* sont parvenu à rassembler les fonds nécessaire pour faire paraître leur feuille"), and "the issue scheduled for February-March left the printing presses at the beginning of April" [Le numéro daté Fev-Mars est sorti des presses de l'imprimeur au début d'Avril].[28]

The newspaper's mission was to address social, political, and economic issues: "*La Dépêche africaine* [is] . . . an independent journal of correspondence between blacks, for the moral and material interests of the indigenous populations, through the objective study of the larger colonial questions considered from political, economic, and social points of view."[29] In this diasporic vein, the periodical infrequently published a section in English titled "United We Stand, Divided We Fall," under the editorship of Fritz Moutia. A staunch Schoelcherist, the editor in chief, Maurice Satineau, wrote a series of articles entitled "Le Schoelcherisme" and announced the creation of a Prix Victor Schoelcher de Littérature Nègrophile in January 1929. Schoelcher was revered by French West Indians, not only because he helped to abolish slavery in the colonies but also for his seemingly progressive political, social, and economic efforts to restructure the colonies into the very image of the metropolis. In directly citing Schoelcher, Satineau writes, "School is the cradle of equality. . . . [T]here must not be any corner of the Island where the child who inhabits it does not find at his door free, secular, and mandatory education."[30] The editor in chief concludes his remarks on

Schoelcher's colonial policies by stating that "he equally considered freedom for the press . . . and universal suffrage [as] the most sure instruments of progress for the colonial populations" (1). Satineau's journal used the ideas of Victor Schoelcher strategically to broach the subject of a new colonial humanism. This humanitarian colonialism, ballyhooed as committed to egalitarianism and uplift through assimilation, is further developed as a necessity to the colonies' ascent into the civilized world in a republished excerpt of an article from *Le Journal de Roubaix* entitled "Elites noires," by Robert Wibaux. Wibaux discusses Africa's evolution and economic development in terms of creating a black elite, a "talented tenth," in Francophone Africa:

> Let us take the case of French West Africa. It is clear that whites cannot uniquely undertake the importance of this immense domain. Too few French, especially among the best, consent to be expatriated. And for those who do, how many fail, discouraged by the rigor of the climate, the complexities of the dialects, of the local morals? The native must help, and if need be replace the white.[31]

Africans should be active participants in the colonial project, in the creation of *evolués*; thus the destruction of local customs, cultures, and traditions. The future elites themselves need first to be evolved, cultivated, fully assimilated in order to assist in Africa's Westernized "evolution." Hence, Wibaux recommends, as part of colonial policy, schools and instruction in Christianity that will help overcome the obstacles that the indigenous culture, with its focus on the collective rather than the individual, poses. Africa will then be saved from "decivilization." France's "fierté" [pride] in Africa will be "justifiée" [justified], and "ce domaine reste notre" [this region will remain French] (1).

La Dépêche africaine also cultivated student involvement and support. In a November 1928 issue, a call out from the Union fédérale des étudiants, a group that attempted to organize "camarades algériens, tunisiens, indochinois, antillais, sénégalais" [Algerian, Tunisian, Indochinese, Antillean, and Senegalese comrades] to address educational inequities between France and their respective countries, was featured:

> You, colonial students, who have suffered from the teaching system set up in your homelands; you to whom one distributes education sparingly; you who must exile yourself to France to look for intellectual nour-

ishment that is systematically denied in your homelands; you must understand that the most fundamental work to be done by you involves your not supporting with not so much as a murmur a state of things prejudicial to your vital interests. But you must to the contrary energetically struggle for your legitimate concerns. Not content to enslave your countries under a brutal yolk, camouflaged under the pompous name "civilization," they have stripped you of all the inherent rights of human nature. When your elders were plunged into the filthy butchery of 1914–1918, they were truly the "sons of France," the "cherished children of the Mother Country." Now that it is a question of your education, you are no longer French, you are merely the "colonized," subjugated by special laws, subjected to particular treatment.[32]

The rather radical tone and strong condemnation of French colonial policy by the student organization represented the militant reformist and assimilationist strand that ran through the columns of *La Dépêche africaine*. The students, like the editors, were not anticolonialists but reformists, intent on compelling France to live up to its humanist ideals. The students recalled the war of 1914–1918 and, in doing so, roused in spirit the militant assimilationist battle cry regarding France's unfulfilled promises to Senegalese and Malagasy soldiers: France has "une dette de sang" [a blood debt].

Delving into Anglophone panblack politics, the organ took on the Scottsboro case in the United States. The Scottsboro case involved nine black men who allegedly raped two white women. Coerced by authorities into giving false statements, the women later retracted their allegations. Seven of the men were nonetheless facing execution when, on April 1, 1932, *La Dépêche africaine* ran a front-page article and letter to President Herbert Hoover. Under the headline "Un suprême appel au président Hoover: L'Exécution des sept nègres serait un crime contre l'humanité," Maurice Satineau and Georges Forgues, president of the CDIRN, appealed thus:

> Profoundly moved by the sentence that the Supreme Court of Alabama is about to hand down against the seven Negroes accused of rape, we are making an appeal to your greater conscience, to your sense of justice, humanity, and equity in order to prevent such an execution which would be considered, by all races and notably, the black race . . . as a crime of which one cannot predict the repercussions.[33]

The official French government response to *La Dépêche africaine* was the dogged monitoring of its editor, Satineau, and the newspaper's contents. With its Pan-Africanist politics as well as the inclusion of Maran and Kojo Tovalou's brother Georges on the editorial board, *La Dépêche africaine* was linked, according to officials, in spirit, politics, and content to *Les Continents* and, by extension, Garveyism; thus, it was a potential threat to the colonial powers of the day. According to one agent's report,

> The address and telephone number are presently those of the management of the journal "La Dépêche africaine." It is thus no longer possible to deny the relations that unite this paper and the pan-black organization. This explains as well why we remarked in the note of last February page 10: "La Dépêche africaine" reminds one of the defunct pan-black organ "Les Continents."[34]

The fact that, after his expulsion from the United States, Garvey set up offices in the seventh arrondissement in Paris at 5 rue Paul Louis Courieur, the same address as *La Dépêche africaine* and with the same telephone number, certainly gave the administration fodder. It was also more than pure coincidence for the colonial administration that *La Dépêche africaine* announced that it would augment publication following Garvey's October 1928 visit: "[L]e journal announce qu'il va devenir bientôt bimensuel: serait-ce une conséquence du passage de Marcus Garvey à Paris?" [The journal announced that it will soon become a bimonthly: is this a consequence of Marcus Garvey's visit to Paris?].[35] Satineau's allusion to Schoelcher's ideas about freedom of the press can be seen perhaps as strategic vis-à-vis government repression, monitoring, and censorship.

Internal divisions also plagued *La Dépêche africaine*. Although some of the collaborators "energetically conformed to Garveyist ideas," others, like Satineau, wanted to strike a balance between furthering Garvey's panblack agenda in order to maintain financial support and currying favor with the colonial administration.[36] In response to being targeted as Garveyite, the management shifted the organ's focus to Guadeloupean politics and began to feature sympathetic articles on colonial administrators, a strategy which government agents regarded as mere camouflage: "The camouflage persists: the portrait of the new minister of colonies is published on the front page with sympathetic commentary."[37] After 1930, the newspaper's political content was viewed less cynically and as nonthreatening to colonial interests. Garveyism, with its glorification of the black race and recognition of ancient African civilizations, less its more troubling racialism; Du Bois's racially imbued Pan-Africanism and musings on double consciousness; and Alain Locke's focus on black self-expression and cultural exploration in *The New Negro*[38] would nonetheless continue to be filtered through a Francophone lens and appropriated in *La Dépêche africaine*'s cultural and literary criticism.

The sections of the newspaper titled "La Dépêche politique," "La Dépêche economique et sociale," and "La Dépêche littéraire" owed their cultural and literary pan-*noirisme* to the global literacy of Mlles Jane and Paulette Nardal. *La Dépêche africaine*'s first issue, in February 1928, presented its prestigious collaborators. A photograph of Jane Nardal listed her qualifications as "Licencée-ès-lettres." Paulette Nardal joined the magazine's roster in June 1928. She was duly titled "Professeur d'Anglais," and her contribution to the journal would be to "write a series of articles on the economic and literary evolution of Black Americans."[39] Paulette Nardal's specialties, however, were more literary and artistic than socioeconomic. Both sisters were Sorbonne-educated, bilingual Martinicans. Their race-conscious transnational finishing school was the salon of René Maran, where they met various African American artists and writers, such as Augusta Savage, Mercer Cook, Alain Locke, Claude McKay, and Langston Hughes. Paulette, the elder of the two, wrote seven pieces for the journal, including one short story; a comparative essay on Antillean and black American music, entitled "Musique nègre: Antilles et AfraAmérique"; and an extensive study, with photographs, of the Harlem Renaissance sculptor Augusta Savage's work.[40] Jane Nardal, for her part, wrote two provocative essays on literary exoticism and black cultural internationalism and coined the neologism *Afro-Latin*. Although their work has been often referred to as "proto-negritude,"[41] and hence as performing a sort of midwifery for the "true" movement, such an assessment is primarily tied to the fact that the word *Negritude* itself would not come into being for at least another eight years. Jane Nardal's "Internationalisme noir" (1928), an essay that discusses race consciousness among the French-speaking African diaspora and cultural *métissage,* would provide the philosophical foundations for Paulette Nardal's 1932 historico-literary essay "L'Éveil de la conscience de race chez les étudiants noirs," Senghorian symbiotic Negritude, and the Césairean "return en soi" of 1935.

2. Jane Nardal: A New Race Spirit and the Francophone New Negro

How strange you were to me that first night. Karukera of raucous syllables, little Africa, mysterious and wild, tight-closed at first, only opening her heart full of simple kindliness to him who already loves her.

—Jane "Yadhé" Nardal, "Le Soir tombe sur Karukera,"
La Revue du monde noir[1]

Henceforth there would be some interest, some originality, some pride in being Negro, in turning back toward Africa, the cradle of Negroes, in remembering a common origin. . . . From these new ideas, new words, whence the creative significance of the terms: Afro-American, Afro-Latin.

—Jane Nardal, "Internationalisme noir," *La Dépêche africaine*

In the "Dépêche économique et sociale" section of the first issue of *La Dépêche africaine,* Jane Nardal's article "Internationalisme noir" appeared. Her name and a summation of her essay as politically "modest" in tone also appeared in a March 1928 agent's report on activities of "Blacks from the colonies in the metropolis."[2] The article outlines in broad-brush strokes several concepts that would become pivotal in early Negritude parlance: *après-guerre nègre,* global community, black internationalism, Afro-Latin, *conscience de race,* French-speaking New Negro, *esprit de race.* In an *après-guerre* commentary, Nardal begins by suggesting that one of the aftereffects of World War I had been an attempt to break down barriers between countries. The peace conference at Versailles as well as the meeting of "four unobtrusive gentlemen" in Paris in 1919 to settle the "destinies of mankind," as W. E. B. Du Bois remarked,[3] under-

score Nardal's observation. Like Du Bois, Nardal links the broader im-
plications of the formation of the Euro-American community after the
war to those of the global black community in formation. If the war led
European and American world powers to envision themselves as a
human community with common interests, it also gave rise to a vague
sentiment among blacks that they too were part of that human community: "[I]n spite of everything they belong to one and the same race."[4]
The renewed spirit of humanism, which weighed heavily in the post-
1918 air that by turns attempted to exclude and marginalize blacks, had
actualized among black elites "un esprit de race" [a race spirit] (5). Although the concept of a unified black race was not novel among those
who helped to construct and shore up the idea, from Buffon to Jefferson
to Gobineau, the subjects of their philosophies of race—blacks—did
not, at least according to Nardal, accept in principle such a notion:

> Previously the more assimilated blacks looked down arrogantly upon
> their colored brethren, believing themselves surely of a different species
> than they; on the other hand, certain blacks who had never left African
> soil to be led into slavery looked down upon as so many base swine
> those who at the whim of whites had been enslaved, then freed, then
> molded into the white man's image. (5)

This Nardalian panorama of schisms among the Francophone African diaspora is a shocking one, underscoring conflict rather than identification.

As Nardal theorizes, World War I and its attendant hardships; the
unfulfilled promises of citizenship and dashed hopes of equal rights; the
presence of black soldiers of various ethnic backgrounds in Europe;
the discovery of *l'art nègre* by European votaries of the "primitive," of
African literature, civilizations, religions, and sculpture; Negro spirituals; and the publication of the philosopher Alain Locke's *The New Negro*
(1925) combined to evoke sentiments of diasporic connectedness and
sentimental glances toward the ancestral homeland of Africa. *The New
Negro,* a volume of collected writings by Negro Renaissance intellectuals, poets, novelists, dramaturges, and cultural critics such as Jessie
Fauset, W. E. B. Du Bois, Jean Toomer, and Georgia Douglass, struck a
resounding chord with Jane Nardal. In his foreword to the anthology,
Locke related that a new "race spirit" among Negroes had emerged on
the American scene, the effect of which had been the emergence of a
New Negro in a New World.[5] *The New Negro,* its editor maintained,

"aims to document the New Negro culturally and socially" (xv). Locke continued:

> Of all the voluminous literature on the Negro, so much is mere external view and commentary that we may warrantably say that nine-tenths of it is *about* the Negro rather than of him, so that it is the Negro problem rather than the Negro that is known and mooted in the general mind. We turn therefore in the other direction to the elements of truest social portraiture, and discover in the artistic self-expression of the Negro to-day a new figure on the national canvas and a new force in the foreground of affairs. (xv)

This New Negro, according to Locke and, later, Nardal, would write him- or herself. Concentrating on self-expression, self-discovery, and cultural reassessment, New Negro writers explored the future of the race in the attendant condition of their Americanism. The New Negro was both a "collaborator and participant in American civilization" and was simultaneously responsible for the safekeeping of race traditions. This New Negro had also developed a "wider race consciousness," recognizing his or her importance on the international canvas, particularly with respect to Africa: "[H]is new internationalism is primarily an effort to recapture contact with the scattered peoples of African derivation. . . . [T]he possible role of the American Negro in the future development of Africa is one of the most constructive and universally helpful missions that any modern people can lay claim to" (14–15).

Guilefully reconceptualizing the New Negro thesis for a Francophone milieu, Nardal tipped the direction toward Africa. Africa was not the European-stereotyped and -promulgated land of savages but a land of rich cultural contrasts and traditions—a continental Mecca, henceforth to be proudly claimed by its Francophone diaspora. From the rubble of enslavement, bestowed freedom in the French West Indies, and the tangle of assimilation, a new consciousness about Africa and race had brought forth the "Afro-Latin." Nardal imagined the merging of Frenchness/Latin-ness and African-ness/blackness into a new identity, a new self-consciousness. The Francophone New Negro would not renounce his or her *latinité* or *africanité*. This symbiosis, synthesis, reconciliation was to bring into existence an authentic self-consciousness. The Afro-Latin shares, then, the experience of the Afro-American, the Du Boisian double consciousness or *double appartenance* [double belonging] in which

one merge[s] his double self into a better and truer self. In this merging
he wishes neither of the older selves to be lost. He would not Africanize
America, for America has too much to teach the world and Africa. He
would not bleach his Negro soul in a flood of white Americanism, for he
knows that Negro blood has a message for the world. He simply wishes
to make it possible for a man to be both a Negro and an American.[6]

Similarly, in its use of the masculinist language of the time as well as
in its philosophic content, "Internationalisme noir" is not merely about
the formation of a global black community or an emergent race consciousness, but about the synergy of the "Afro" or African and the Latin
world, an embracing of cultural *métissage,* of *double appartenance,* in
order to return "en soi":

> From these new ideas, new words, whence the creative significance
> of the terms: Afro-American, Afro-Latin. They confirm our thesis while
> casting new meaning on the nature of this Black Internationalism. If the
> Negro wants to know himself, assert his personality, and not be the copy
> of this or that type from another race (which often earns him contempt
> and mockery), it does not follow from that, however, that he becomes
> resolutely hostile to all contributions made by another race. On the con-
> trary, he must learn to profit from others' acquired experience and in-
> tellectual wealth, but in order to know himself better and to assert his
> personality. To be Afro-American, to be Afro-Latin, means to be an en-
> couragement, a consolation, an example for the blacks of Africa by
> showing them that certain benefits of white civilization do not neces-
> sarily lead to a rejection of one's race.
>
> Africans, on the other hand, could profit from this example by rec-
> onciling these teachings with the millennial traditions of which they are
> justly proud.[7]

Nardal's cultural mixing does not dismiss African traditions or reserve for Africa the gift of emotion versus reason—a racialist distortion
of her theorizing that would later crop up in Senghor's "L'Humanisme et
nous" and *Liberté 1: Négritude et humanisme.* Her fatalism, if you will,
emerges around the French colonial project. However, she calls for symbiosis as a path of cultural and racial resistance to passive assimilation.
The Afro will assimilate the Latin rather than be wholly assimilated by
it. Yet hostility to "une autre race," an allusion to strident interpretations

of Garveyist thinking, clearly undermines the new humanist spirit that she attempts to outline. The return to the self, the excavation of the glories of the black race with European critical tools of engagement, allows for a better understanding of who one is as "black" and "French," "Afro" and "Latin."

In keeping with the benefits of the colonialism ideology of *La Dépêche africaine* and clearly in the mode of *The New Negro*'s integrationist agenda, Nardal shifts the concept of *afro-latinité* from the West Indian frame of reference to the Franco-African terrain, where mass indigenous resistance had proven most formidable. Versed in the ethnological and sociological literature of the day on Africa—Maurice Delafosse, Leo Frobenius, and Jean Price-Mars—Nardal writes that "the cultivated man" would not treat the Africans "en masse as savages," because "[t]he work of sociologists has made known to the white world the centers of African civilization, their religious systems, their forms of government, their artistic wealth" (5). Although sympathetic to the "bitterness" [amertume] that Africans express in seeing the effects of colonization on these "millénaire" traditions, she argues conversely that colonial policy in Africa could be a source of racial "solidarity" and race consciousness among the different African "tribes" (5).

She further offers up Afro-Americans as pioneers of resistance, cultural innovation, preservation, and race consciousness blended with their fierce Americanism, suggesting to her Francophone readers that they immerse themselves in *The New Negro*. The combined socioeconomic, political, and historical realities of black life under the yoke of American racism have contributed to the emergence of Afro-American cultural expressions that speak to such singular experiences and chronicle the coming-into-being of the New Negro. For Nardal, without the one—the hardships of those experiences as marginalized Americans—there would not be the other: a race-conscious New American Negro. French-speaking blacks, Afro-Latins, "in contact with a race less hostile to the man of color than the Anglo-Saxon race, have been for that reason retarded in this path" of race consciousness, "authentic" cultural development, and race solidarity (5). The Afro-American will, for Nardal, serve as a model for the Afro-Latin, for Afro-Latin literature, and art— culture as the archive and simulacrum of social processes and history— as such are nonexistent. Nardal encourages the Afro-Latin to recognize that Africa and "le pays latin" are not "incompatibles" (5). She wants nothing less than a Francophone Negro Renaissance. She prophesies the coming-into-being of Francophone New Negroes, of "jeunes Afro-Latins" [young Afro-Latins] who, "schooled in European methods" and "aidés, encouragés par les intellectuels noir américains, se séparant de la génération précedente . . . [et] formés aux méthodes européenes, ils s'en serviront pour étudier l'esprit de leur race, le passé de leur race, avec tout l'esprit critique nécessaire" [helped, encouraged by black American intellectuals . . . (are) distinguishing themselves from the preceding generation . . . to study the spirit of their race, the past of their race with all the necessary critical verve] (5).

As Promethean around issues of identity and race in the black Francophone context as Nardal's concepts of *afro-latinité* and cultural *métissage* were in 1928, they were also importantly subversive; indeed, they went philosophically counter to the universalism supposedly inherent in French humanism, culture, and colonial policies on "nos colonies et nos indigènes." Nardal suggests a decentering of Frenchness. Yet, for France, the essence of the words *culture* and *civilization is* Frenchness, France. With sword and/or gun in hand, France imparts the "souveraineté de ses lois et la marque de son génie" [the sovereignty of its laws and the mark of its genius] to the conquered.[8] The French will "do them [the natives] good in spite of themselves" through the gift of Frenchness.[9] In his *L'Introduction à l'histoire universelle*, Jules Michelet characterized the French as indulging in "ardent proselytizing" in their objective of assimilating the vanquished to the universal that is France:

> The Frenchman wants above all to imprint his personality on the vanquished, not as his own, but as the quintessence of the good and the beautiful; this is his naive belief. He believes that he could do nothing more beneficial for the world than to give it his ideas, customs, ways of doing things. He will convert other peoples to these ways sword in hand, and after the battle, in part smugly and in part sympathetically, he will reveal to them all that they gain by becoming French. Do not laugh; those who invariably want to make the world in their image, finish by doing so. . . . Each one of our armies, upon retreating, has left behind a France.[10]

Ideas of difference, integration, symbiosis, synergy, syncretization, and hyphenations were threatening to *l'esprit français nationale,* to the body politic, the belief in the "plus grande France."[11] Despite Nardal's advocating a racial identity politics for specifically cultural purposes, politically such a race-conscious politics would prove to be the bane of French colonialism in Africa, for it would set in motion the historical processes of decolonization. Was Nardal aware at the time of the insurgent subtext of her black humanism and cultural panblackness? Years later, she and her sister Paulette would insist on their unique intentions to create a cultural, not political, movement similar to that of the New Negro in America.[12] "Internationalisme noir," however, with its somewhat embellished and "ardent proselytizing" résumé of a nascent race consciousness among Afro-Latins, which would lead to a cultural explosion à la Afro-American mode—that is, to Negritude—interestingly maps out the first stage in the dialectics of liberation for the colonized. Such a politically charged stand would arouse government suspicions and would shadow the two sisters in their future cultural collaboration: a bilingual review.

Jane Nardal's last contribution to *La Dépêche africaine* appeared in October of the same year, 1928, in the "Dépêche politique" section of the journal. In a literary tour de force, Nardal takes on exoticism in French letters, crosses the Atlantic for a comparative discussion of Harriet Beecher Stowe's *Uncle Tom's Cabin* and the modernist reconfigurations in Carl Van Vechten's best-seller *Nigger Heaven,* and concludes with an ascerbic critique of *indigénophile* French writer Paul Morand's *Magie noire.* Jane Nardal was not the only black Francophone intellectual sufficiently perturbed by *Magie noire* to write an editorial. In the October 1928 issue of *La Race nègre,* an editorial entitled "La Trahison du clerc Paul Morand" was printed. Borrowing title and substance from the philosopher Julien Benda's tract *La Trahison des clercs,* the writer suggests that the intellectual's social role is to "enlighten people, guide the masses toward an ideal existence." The intellectual betrays his social responsibility when "in a word . . . he places his spiritual authority in the service of an unjust collective cause."[13] From the point of view of Jane Nardal and the anonymous *La Race nègre* critic, Morand had performed such a treachery. But Nardal's essay, in its very erudition and literateness, demonstrates the continuity of the exoticist motif in French and American literature, whereby the *nègre* functions as a puppet, assuming various stereotyped guises for an America and Europe in crisis. In an era rife with primitivist art exhibitions and Josephine

Bakermania—an "age de nègre," as Morand writes[14]—Nardal's essay intones a sobering and critical note. Rather than reveling in the attention given to things and persons black, as many writers, artists, and members of the black intelligentsia did in their quest for influential white patronage, Jane Nardal is concerned with questions of race and representation in modern culture and humanism. "Pantins exotiques," or "Exotic Puppets," as her final commentary is titled, begins by drawing upon its black Francophone reader's myriad experiences with the labyrinth of French exoticism:

> Regarding the evocative power of certain words, the Creole who has spent time in France can readily testify. Should it come to be known or perceived that you are "exotic," you will arouse a lively interest, preposterous questions, the dreams and regrets of those who have never traveled: "Oh! The golden Islands! the marvelous lands! with their happy, naive, carefree natives!"[15]

Nardal presents two courses of action for the exoticized: gratefully accept the exoticism, as most will do, or courageously enter upon the landscape of humanity and trample the interlocutor's vision of a "rococo decor of hammocks, palm trees, virgin forests," and "exotic princesses" by disclosing, like any "petite bourgeoise française," that "you are in Paris pursuing studies that you began over there, in the Tropics, in high school" (2). Exoticism, Nardal further informs the reader, a mainstay of the metropolitan literary imagination vis-à-vis the colonies, has thoroughly impregnated the social imagination.

On the listless tour from the enticing, far-flung lands described by Bernardin de Saint-Pierre and the "bon sauvage" for humanitarian causes à la Michelet, Hugo, and Stowe to the *véritable nègre* poetics of early colonialist writers like Conrad and Leblond, we are compelled by way of Nardal's narrative to make a screeching and lengthy stop at French cultural icon Josephine Baker and her American *bal nègre* colleagues:

> But Josephine came, Josephine Baker you understand, and bored a hole through the painted backdrop associated with Bernardin. Here it is that a woman of color leaps onstage with her shellacked hair and sparkling smile. She is certainly still dressed in feathers and banana leaves, but she brings to Parisians the latest Broadway products (the Charleston, jazz, etc.). The transition between past and present, the soldering

between virgin forest and modernism, is what American blacks have accomplished and rendered tangible.

And the blasé artists and snobs find in them what they seek: the savorous, spicy contrast of primitive beings in an ultramodern frame of African frenzy unfurled in the cubist decor of a nightclub. This explains the unprecedented vogue and the swell of enthusiasm generated by a little *capresse* who was begging on the sidewalks of St. Louis (Mississippi) *[sic]*.

For she and her friends . . . in the course of entertaining the Parisian public, offer new and truculent images for the avant-garde writers. In hearing their sweet and raucous melodies in concert, in the music hall, on records, these writers reconstitute a strange atmosphere where one still hears something reminiscent of the wailing of poor slaves with an aftertaste of naïveté and now and then savagery. Thus, in modern, exotic literature, the poetic imagination loses none of its prerogatives, even when it no longer awards the prize for excellence to good "Uncle Toms."[16]

With a litany of adjectives, Nardal explores and explains Baker's cultural currency in 1920s Paris. The American New Negro represented for the French a detour not only from the ennui of whiteness but also from Francophone black *métropolitains* and *indigènes* in Africa and the West Indies who had been, as René Maran wrote, "shaped into their own image."[17] As part of the Jazz Age, Baker was found everywhere, inspiring films and whetting the imagination of the *indigénophiles,* as French writers of this exotic literary genre were aptly called. She represented the spontaneity, innocence, and naturalness lost to this civilizing and civilized French nation because of its obsession with modern techniques. She was blackness with verve. As historian Tyler Stovall writes, "When the French looked at black Americans, they saw a new version of the sensuous, spontaneous African."[18] *Indigénophile* literature was a blend of racially charged stereotypes—blacks as primitive, sexually licentious, savage—and, more often than not, paternalism. The theme of atavism was de rigueur, whether in the exoticism of the Bernardin and Stowe ilk or in Van Vechten and the surrealist Philippe Soupault's gritty renditions of black urban life. Van Vechten's Anatole Longfellow, alias Scarlet Creeper, and Morand's Congo had merely replaced Stowe's Uncle Tom and Claire de Duras's Ourika. As Nardal writes, "So, after the grenadine syrup of Bernardin and Beecher Stowe, here are the hard liquor and cocktails of Soupault, of Carl Van Vechten: Cover your face, Uncle Tom, up there; here is your grandson Edgar Manning, the hero of Soupault's novel."[19] Soupault's *Le Nègre,* reviewed in the June 15, 1928, issue of *La Dépêche africaine* as negrophilic and sincere,[20] and Van Vechten's *Nigger Heaven* shared essentially, as Nardal remarks, "these same character types and vices,"[21] whereas Morand's *Magie noire* and Van Vechten's *Nigger Heaven* were somewhat parasitic, with the former leeching themes from the latter and Van Vechten referring reverently to Morand in his novel.[22]

Carl Van Vechten, patron of the Harlem Renaissance movement and confidant of writer Nella Larsen, published his best-seller *Nigger Heaven* in August 1926. The work went into a sixth printing by October of the same year. Set primarily in Harlem, which many of the characters refer to as "nigger heaven," the novel pirouettes around a love story of tortured proportions between Mary Love, a respectable, well-educated young woman, and Byron Kasson, an Ivy-league-educated, sexually insatiable aspiring writer. Surrounding the ill-fated pair is a varied cast of characters like the gigolo Scarlet Creeper; the gambler Randolph Pettijohn, the Bolito King; the once widely acclaimed stage performer Adora; the licentious, coke-snorting, man-eating Lasca Sartoris; the upper-class Sumners; and the socially respectable Olive Hamilton and Howard Allison. Van Vechten fills the work with "Negro" slang of the era, offering a glossary of terms in the back of the book, "authentic dialect," and images of white voyeurs watching gyrating, in-heat black bodies in uptown clubs. Covering such issues as "passing" and the schisms between Du Bois's "from-above" talented-tenth concept and the folk preoccupations of the Negro Renaissance on the question of race and literary representation,[23] Van Vechten's authentic Negro artistry essentially rests on a barrage of stereotypes. There is a risqué nightspot called the Black Venus, which functions as a metaphor for sensual black female sexuality. The upcoming wedding of Howard and Olive is referred to as "more than a marriage; it was a primitive consecration."[24]

There is also a soliloquy on the passionate nature of blacks as it relates to crime:

> Negroes never premeditate murder; their murders are committed under
> the reign of passion. If one made a temporary escape from a man bent
> on killing, it was likely to prove a permanent escape. The next morning,
> in another mood, probably he would have forgotten his purpose. There

never had been . . . a Negro poisoner. Negroes use instruments that deal
death swiftly: knives, razors, revolvers. (90)

Premeditation requires calculation and planning—something the passionate and, importantly, fickle Negro, who quickly forgets why he was
bent on killing over the course of a night's sleep, is incapable of carrying
out. Slow deaths—like those accompanied by poison—are also not characteristic of the Negro's nature; rather, Negroes like death like they like
all things: quick and easy. Patience is, quite frankly, not a Negro virtue.

Our brown-skinned heroine, Mary, who has somehow been unable
to tap into her savage birthright until she meets Byron, offers a most enduring portrait of the nature of this primitive race for Van Vechten's predominantly white readers:

> Savages! Savages at heart! And she had lost or forfeited her birthright,
> this primitive birthright which was so valuable and important an asset, a
> birthright that all civilized races were struggling to get back to—this fact
> explained the art of Picasso or a Stravinsky. To be sure, she, too, felt this
> African beat—it completely aroused her emotionally—but she was con-
> scious of feeling it. This love of drums, of exciting rhythms, this naïve
> delight in glowing colour—the colour that exists only in cloudless, tropi-
> cal climes—this warm, sexual emotion . . . (89–90)

Mary eventually recovers, or uncovers (as the black is naturally prone to
atavism), this birthright that has been repressed from years of being
steeped in the literature and the arts of the white Western world. Her relationship with Byron, a being thoroughly in touch with his sexuality,
draws out a range of Negro emotions in Mary, namely agonizing, passionate devotion and Othello-like jealousy.

If only for their diasporic and cartographic range, Paul Morand's
tales in *Magie noire* surpass Van Vechten's exotic tableaux. *Magie noire*
emerged on the *indigènophile* literary radar in 1928. The novel was later
translated into English as *Black Magic* with the help of writer and
NAACP official Walter White and was published in 1929 by Viking.
Like an ethnographer presenting his travelogues, Morand notes in the
opening of the book that "50,000 kilometers and 28 Negro countries"
have informed his novellas, which traverse Haiti, France, and various
parts of the United States and sub-Saharan Africa. The author relies
heavily as well on the *La Mentalité primitive* of Lucien Lévy-Bruhl for

his rendition of African ways of knowing, Van Vechten's *Nigger Heaven,* and, as Nardal suspects, a distorted appropriation of Alain Locke's *The New Negro* for his perspectives on black Americans. Morand presents the reader with the miserable Haitian mulatto Occide, who succeeds in becoming tsar of Haiti; the wealthy black American Pamela Freedman, who passes as white only to return to Africa and go primitive; the Parisian dancer Congo, who is consumed by voodoo; Octavius Bloom and his family of Louisiana Creoles, who try unsuccessfully to "pass" as white because the white skin of Bloom's sister gradually begins to turn brown; a blackphobic white female Southerner who, acting upon her sexually repressed desires for black men, causes a lynching by white Americans in the south of France; the legend of African cannibalism; and a derisive rendering of the New Negro in Dr. Lincoln Vamp. In describing the dancer Congo, Morand writes:

> [She is] eighteen years old, and has been dancing for eighteen years. She is a freak of nature. But her principal gift is not really her dancing, nor her comical powers, nor her exotic grace, nor the grimaces that distort her features. . . . No, it is simply instantaneous transmission of her immense vitality, the discharge of a current more violent than the electric chairs. . . . And Paris laughs its tired, cynical laugh, ingratiated by the primitive merriness of these lively limbs, cheered by these stone-aged gambolings, its blood quickened by this organic, unquenchable radiance: can she be ignorant of God's gift to the Negroes of His most priceless treasure—the gift of Joy?[25]

In a thinly disguised allusion to Josephine Baker, Morand has a character remark, "She reminds me of Josephine. . . . No not that one—I mean the Josephine who used to be Empress long ago" (7). (Interestingly, Marie-Josèphe Rose Tascher de la Pagerie, renamed Joséphine by her beloved Napoleon, was born on the island of Martinique. Like both Congo and Josephine Baker, Joséphine was an import to France. She was Creole, a Frenchwoman born in the New Francophone World, and a lubricious one at that, who, as biographer Carolly Erickson writes, enjoyed dancing and the occult and held salons. Because of her exotic *pays natal,* she was known as the "little American" at her salons held at Penthémont in Paris during 1784.)[26] And, of course, Congo is Josephine Baker. Congo's popularity, like Baker's, is her ability to inspire joy in war-weary, mechanized Paris, to take Parisians back to a time of "idyllic creatures," white innocence, and "faraway lands where everything is vibrantly afire: air, hearts, bodies."[27]

In Morand's third short story, "Adieu New York," the American gentleman who reveals Pamela Freedman's "passing" to the other passengers on a whites-only cruise ship bound for Africa relates:

> I felt she had something more than white blood. . . . And after all what would happen if Blacks did contrive to be white? . . . But seriously . . . our age is a Negro age. Just think of the general slackness, the distaste of the young for hard work, the nudity on the Lido or at Palm Beach, equality, fraternity, clay houses that last three years, public love-making, divorce, publicity. . . . In fact, the Negro is just our own shadow![28]

The black is excess, "something more" than the white but always beside the white, tracking the white like a shadow. The black represents the underbelly of white civilization, the darker face of Janus. If whiteness is innocence, blackness is "public love-making"; if whiteness is industriousness, blackness is "general slackness." One cannot escape the black, just as one cannot escape one's shadow. And certainly in a dangerous reversal of the assimilation process, the white has assimilated to the black way of life. Pamela's "contriving" to be white is simply a concerted effort to merge the shadow into the white self, as often happens when the sun does not refract the shadow—the two, shadow and white, meet as one. Nardal adroitly infers from the American gentleman's commentary on the "age de nègre" that "[w]e have here not the portrait of the Negro, but that of the postwar European [or American] assimilated to the Negro." There is a moralizing tone in Morand's novella, a desire to invoke "shame" from this Europe and America in crisis. There is a struggle between the black and white for the white Western world's soul.[29] In the end, at least according to Morand's racial formula, everyone falls perfectly into place. Pamela, intoxicated by the drums, the chants, and the magic of the African natives, decides that "she has had enough of being a phony white woman" and returns "to the state of savagery."[30]

For Morand, Nardal writes, "the power of Negro atavism" is omnipresent and inescapable: "Whatever he be, black or almost white, well-schooled or illiterate, French, American, or in a state of savagery, in short, civilized in appearance, the Negro, if the occasion permits, will return to his instincts."[31] Nardal weds the exotic motifs of literary blackness to the *vogue nègre* of the era, in which blacks have become "destined to serve as amusement, to see to the pleasure, artistic or sensual, of whites" (2). Caught between the exoticism of old, with its often humanitarian twists, and this new "realist" version, she poses a rhetorical question to her black readers: "With which sauce do we want to be eaten: the idealist sauce or the realist one?" (2). Aesthetic pleasure—clearly profitable, as the popularity and sales figures of Morand's work attest—rather than a veritable engagement with the Negro, makes for an impoverished art and humanism. As Nardal suggests, "[W]hen it is a question of intellectual, or moral, qualities, when it is a question of no longer being their clown but their equal, that disturbs nature's plan and the viewpoints of providence. Thus, for aesthetic pleasure, Paul Morand and his consorts rely on or return to the state of nature, like Ms. Pamela Freedman" (2).

Nardal concludes "Pantins exotiques" by calling for a more complex rendering of literary blackness by French and American writers, one that will allow the Negro "to enter into the human community" (2). In essence, she implores the modernist literati to expand their notion of humanity, to recognize the complex humanity of the black—an awesome philosophical commitment for writers like Morand and Van Vechten, fustian puppeteers incessantly pulling the strings of literary Negro marionettes to articulate their desires and anxieties. Jane Nardal did not yet make a direct call for a race-conscious literature by Antilleans to counteract regressive American and European representations, as Antilleans in 1928 had yet to fully come to terms with their fragmented identities as Afro-Latin and their fragile relationship to Africa. That call would emerge some three years later with the founding of *La Revue du monde noir.*

3. Les Soeurs Nardal and the Clamart Salon: Content and Context of *La Revue du monde noir,* 1931–1932

By 1931, France, particularly the capital, Paris, had come to be regarded as a culturally vibrant safe haven of sorts by many members of the African American political, literary, and artistic communities. Josephine Baker was performing at the Casino de Paris and the Folies Bergères, and Langston Hughes, Claude McKay, Countee Cullen, Alain Locke, Jessie Redmon Fauset Harris, and Nella Larsen could be seen about at cafés and lunch parties and frequenting the various salons in the 1930s. In addition, 1931 was the year of the Exposition Coloniale at the Bois de Vincennes in Paris, where the colonies were, for some, like the Surrealist Group, perversely showcased, given the abuses and exploitative capitalist nature of the colonial project. With its pictures, artworks, drawings, and documents, the exposition was, in the view of the French government, a celebration of "la plus grande France," a "New France" undaunted in its civilizing missions by geographical boundaries. Intrigued and prideful citizens from all over France and visitors from abroad attended the exposition, held from May to November.

On the eve of all this cultural activity in Paris, the Sunday salon at 7 rue Hébert in Clamart, a suburb of the capital, began. Its hosts were Andrée, Jane, and Paulette Nardal. Drinking *thé à l'anglaise* and speaking in French and English, the hosts and their guests danced; discussed interracial and colonial problems, racist injustices, and current events; examined the precarious position of men and women of color in the metropolis; and, ironically, reveled in the attention to things and persons black generated by the Colonial Exposition.[1] For these *evolués*, the exposition was an affirmation of black cultural expression, as African artwork, music, and such were lauded in grandiose displays. No longer could the contributions of Africa, that "dark continent" from which they were all descended, to the world of culture be denied.

Louis Achilles, a cousin of the Nardal sisters, described the unpretentious setting and intellectual atmosphere of the Clamart salon:

> They were discovering a common manner of being, of feeling, of hoping and soon, of acting! Incapable for the most part of recovering common African roots, they simply called themselves "Black." . . . A feminine influence set the tone and the rites of these convivial afternoons as opposed to a corporate circle or a masculine club. The furniture in the two rooms of these exchanges, the living and dining rooms, bore no resemblance in decor to a traditional bourgeois French or even Antillean salon. Some English easy chairs, airy, comfortable, and light, facilitated the conversation. . . . Not wine, beer, French cider, whisky, exotic coffee, nor Creole punch refreshed one's throat. Tea with milk alone was sipped at these meetings that did not go beyond the hour of dinner and were adjusted to the Paris train schedule.[2]

Achilles delineates the expressly feminized and familial milieu of the Clamart salon. In this salon, where three cultivated women perfected *l'art civilisateur,* women and men, blacks and whites, French, Africans, and Americans exchanged ideas. Held in the building where all three sisters lived, from the oldest, Paulette, to the youngest, Andrée, a student, the intense intellectual dialogue on humanism, literature, art, *actualités,* and the future of the Negro race resembled in spirit the ancien régime salons of Mmes de Tencin and du Deffand. Among salons of French-speaking blacks, the Clamart salon was the only one hosted by Martinican women. The Nardals' transracial, ethnically diverse, and gender-inclusive salon certainly demonstrated a progressiveness that the Left Bank salons set up by white American women expatriates who had fled the puritanism of American culture failed to acquire in the 1930s. The salons of women like Natalie Barney and Gertrude Stein in some respects replicated the race/gender divide they left in America. Barney set up a "formal," essentially white feminist colony that transcended class, and Stein preferred to cultivate relations with a predominantly male French and American expatriate community in her "casual" Parisian salon.[3] In effect, black women were generally excluded on both counts.

The cultural and racial discussions taking place at Clamart were also occurring in Paris in the surrealist milieu nurtured by wealthy British expatriate Nancy Cunard. Cunard's initial interests in black music and sculpture were further broadened through her romantic involvement with black American musician Henry Crowder. Their relationship and discussions provided Cunard with a more intimate understanding of racial discrimination. This intensified interest spurred her to assemble a collection of contemporary black writings. In April 1931, Cunard circulated a flyer with a letter requesting contributions for a volume tentatively titled *Color:*

> The new book *COLOR* here described comprises what is Negro and descended from Negro. . . . It will be entirely *Documentary*. . . . I want outspoken criticism, comment, and comparison from the Negro on the present-day civilizations of Europe, America, South America, the West Indies, African Colonies, etc. . . . This is the first time such a book has been compiled in this manner. It is primarily for Colored people and it is dedicated to one of them. I wish by their aid to make it possible.[4]

Cunard's initial title may be owing to the influence of Countee Cullen's first book of poetry, *Color,* published in 1925. The Cunard project was eventually retitled *Negro: An Anthology,* published in 1934, and dedicated to Henry Crowder, Cunard's "first Negro friend." Its contributors were among the twentieth century's foremost literary luminaries. Zora Neale Hurston, Alain Locke, W. E. B. Du Bois, Jacques Roumain, Nicolás Guillen, Ezra Pound, and Samuel Beckett all appeared within the voluminous anthology's pages. Andrée Nardal also responded to the flyer's call. *Negro* includes very little on the Francophone Antilles. Nardal's essay "The Beguine of the French Antilles" is a reprinted version of her article originally titled "Étude sur la Biguine Créole," which appeared in *La Revue du monde noir* in December 1931. Published under the nom de plume "Madiana" in *Negro,* an allusion perhaps to the original name given Martinique by the Carib Indians—Madinina—the essay offers up a rather vivid analysis of the bodily gestures, syncopation, rhythmic tempo, and humorous yet raw language of the folk songs that accompany the Creole dance the beguine. Although it had been popularized by Josephine Baker in *Paris qui remue,* Nardal objected to its rather vulgar reinterpretation in Parisian dance halls. The Franco–West Indian dance, she wrote, "express[es] a languorous grace and an extreme liveliness [that] mimic the everlasting pursuit of woman by man."[5] With its attention to dance and music, Nardal's essay rounds out the socio-cultural objectives of both Cunard's *Negro* and *La Revue du monde noir.*

It was, importantly, at the convivial Clamart salon that the idea for a monthly bilingual, multiracial collaborative review was conceived. Under the collective editorial management of the *soeurs* Nardal; Haitian scholar Léo Sajous, a specialist on Liberian issues; the bilingual black American educator Clara Shepard; and Louis-Jean Finot, described in one police report as "a dangerous Negrophile married to a black violinist," *La Revue du monde noir* was launched in the fall of 1931.[6] Its title serves as a link to both the Pan-African Congress's proposed monthly, *Black Review,* of which the three sisters were aware, and Garvey's *Negro World.* Paulette Nardal, who served as general secretary, edited, translated, and formatted the review with the help of Clara Shepard.[7] The offices for *La Revue* were located at 45 rue Jacob, on the Left Bank. According to Paulette Nardal, "This review, this movement, it was something that had to happen. It happened like that, like a sudden dawning. At that time, people were ready to read such a review."[8] Moreover, there was then no competing bilingual, panblack literary or cultural magazine in France or imported from the United States; even Dorothy West's *Challenge,* though diasporic in some of its content, was not bilingual. The Nardals' review differed from its Francophone predecessors primarily in that it was more a literary, sociological, and cultural entity than a political vehicle with limited cultural commentary. It was, quite plainly, a "review," and not a newspaper or *journal,* in the French sense of the word. *La Revue's* uniqueness lay also in its objective to cultivate minds that would produce cultural artifacts and aesthetics out of the sociocultural situation of blackness. In effect, *La Revue du monde noir* endeavored to inspire creative dialogue and the exchange of ideas between and among the African diaspora that would ultimately launch, at least as Paulette Nardal contends in "L'Éveil de la conscience de race chez les étudiants noirs" (1932), an authentic literary movement in the black Francophone world.[9] The first issue of the review appeared in October 1931. Its global objectives were boldly declared in a piece called "Our Aim," stating "ce que nous voulons faire":

> To give to the intelligentsia of the black race and their partisans an official organ in which to publish their artistic, literary and scientific works.

To study and to popularize, by means of the press, books, lectures, courses, all which concerns NEGRO CIVILIZATION and the natural riches of Africa, thrice sacred to the black race.

The triple aim which LA REVUE DU MONDE NOIR will pursue, will be: to create among the Negroes of the entire world, regardless of nationality, an intellectual, and moral tie, which will permit them to better know each other, to love one another, to defend more effectively their collective interests, and to glorify their race.

By this means, the Negro race will contribute, along with thinking minds of other races and with all those who have received the light of truth, beauty, and goodness, to the material, the moral, and the intellectual improvement of humanity.

The motto is and will continue to be:

For PEACE, WORK, and JUSTICE.

By LIBERTY, EQUALITY, and FRATERNITY.

Thus, the two hundred million individuals which constitute the Negro race, even though scattered among the various nations, will form over and above the latter a great Brotherhood, the forerunner of universal Democracy.[10]

With its ambitious mission, the collective sought out and published articles, book reviews, poetry, short stories, editorials, and letters to the editor in a section called the "Negroes' Letterbox" on a variety of topics relating to Africa and the diaspora in Cuba, the United States, Liberia, Ethiopia, and the Francophone Antilles. Articles such as "The Problem of Work in Haiti," "The Negroes and Art," "Reflections on Islam," and "The Negro in Cuba"; editorials titled "Justice in America," referring to the Scottsboro case; reprints of ethnologist Leo Frobenius's "Spiritism in Central Africa"; novelistic extracts by Walter White; and poetry by Claude McKay, René Maran, and Langston Hughes appeared within its pages. And, as in *The New Negro,* drawings by Harlem Renaissance artist Aaron Douglas appeared in the first issue of *La Revue du monde noir.*

The early *Revue* included, as well, an interesting dialogue titled "How Should Negroes Living in Europe Dress?" in the "Question Corner." The discussion around blacks and European fashion was broached in the review's second issue. The French philosopher Henri Bergson's *Le Rire: Essai sur la signification du comique* served as the impetus for the discussion. Bergson pondered the question of why blacks who dressed in

European clothing provoked laughter from whites ("Pourquoi la vue d'un Noir habillé à l'européene provoque-t-elle le rire du Blanc?"). Bergson responded to his own query: "Because the white man thinks the Negro is disguised."[11] The deeper philosophical issue presented by Bergson's inquiry and response involves identity and authenticity. The editors frankly rephrased the question as "How should Negroes living in Europe dress?" and enlisted their readers and some contributors to respond. The respondents took up the issues of identity, nationalism, colonialism, authenticity, and Europe as a universal culture. As Louis Achilles offered in his rejoinder in the third issue, in 1932, "How should Negroes in Europe dress? In their national costumes? Of course not, because some them cannot be worn in European climates and furthermore, many Negroes have no national dress other than the European ones."[12]

The review received part of its funding from the Ministry of the Colonies; hence, subjects of an overtly political nature were expressly to be avoided. As Paulette Nardal remarked in a November 1963 letter to Senghor biographer Jacques Louis Hymans: "We only felt the need of bringing back the Negro into the human community and of getting him to rid himself of his complexes. . . . Our preoccupations were of a racial, literary, and artistic order."[13] As a witness to the fates of both *Les Continents* and *La Dépêche africaine* and its editors after they entered the political arena—René Maran was sued in court for defamation of character because of an inflammatory critique of Blaise Diagne, resulting in the financial collapse of *Les Continents*; and Maurice Satineau was doggedly pursued as being "contre les autorités blanche partout" [against white authority everywhere][14]—Paulette Nardal concluded that politics was too dangerous. Thus, the cultural and sociological emphasis of *La Revue du monde noir* led critics, among them Marxist-surrealist poet Étienne Léro (who had contributed to the review) and Aimé Césaire (who had read it with enthusiasm as a student and frequented the Clamart salon) to characterize the review as "rose water," apolitical, bourgeois, and assimilationist.[15] Ironically, Leopold Senghor's Negritude—particularly the call for a new black literature, the rehabilitation of Africa and black values, black humanism, and cultural *métissage*—was indebted to *La Revue* and, more specifically, to the race writings of Jane and Paulette Nardal.[16] The charge of apoliticism is also fraught with contradictions, as Césaire, Senghor, and Damas expressly avoided politics in the 1930s: "To the handful of young French West Indians who cried out in the name of communism, 'Politics first,' we replied, 'Culture first.' We must promote *négritude*."[17]

As *La Revue du monde noir*'s aim states, the publication targeted a particular class of blacks and their "partisans": the elites of other races. The articles found within the review's six issues, specifically those written by Antilleans on the Antillean situation vis-à-vis French culture, clearly advocate a democratic collaboration between Western culture and the black world. The notion of a total abandonment of white Western culture for all things African represents, for Paulette Nardal, a return to "obscurantism," to the unknown. Moreover, she is not interested in declaring "war upon Latin culture and the white world in general."[18] Yet the review's very presence on the cultural scene as an instrument through which to "glorify [blacks'] race" and "defend their collective interests" challenged French cultural and white racial hegemony. Though the review naively assumed that all African-descended people, or at least those members of the black intelligentsia to which the publication was directed, had common interests, its goals were to globalize Negro consciousness and to create a Negro humanism. "Our Aim" rejected passive assimilation in favor of an integration, or appropriation, of white Western culture and this New Negro culture that, in the words of Alain Locke, a frequent visitor to the Clamart salon, "rebuilt [the Negro] past to build his future" for "the material, the moral, and the intellectual improvement of humanity."[19] Notwithstanding an article by Swedish anthropologist H. M. Bernelot-Moens on the "unscientific" demarcation of individuals in the United States according to race,[20] the black writers never challenged the social and legal construction of racial categories as a means of pursuing humanistic ends. Rather, they proudly donned the mantle of Negroness and endeavored to affirm the Negro's being in the world through cultural, artistic, and scientific works. Using the rhetoric of *les droits de l'homme,* of liberty, equality, and fraternity and the principles of the Enlightenment—"light of truth, beauty, goodness"—to foreground their racial Pan-Africanism, the editors of *La Revue du monde noir* further ventured to shape this new Negro humanism from enlightened minds of all races in order to displace the specious model of universal humanism and democracy that was implicitly white. It is, then, no small wonder that the French police and colonial administrators, believing the contributors had ties at various moments to Communists and American Garveyites, kept abreast of the activities of the review's contributors,[21] and that the review, plagued by funding issues after colonial administrators withheld further monetary support, "brutally" ceased publication after a mere six issues, as Louis Achilles writes.[22]

Like J. Edgar Hoover's FBI during the same era, the French government was forever on the lookout for Communist leanings among members of the black Francophone community in the metropolis and indeed saw Communism, even when it did not manifest itself, at nearly every opportunity. The charge of Garveyism, however, had a tripartite origin: the cultural and racial Pan-Africanism advocated by the review sometimes bled into the political; both Jane and Paulette Nardal wrote for the Garvey-linked newspaper *La Dépêche africaine,* and Paulette continued to write articles for the organ while she simultaneously edited and wrote for *La Revue du monde noir;* more importantly, an article on Liberia by Léo Sajous in the December 1931 issue of the review praised Garveyism. The latter article, "Les Noirs Américains au Liberia," begins by attempting to correct an erroneous report by the International Commission regarding the Liberian policy on black American immigration.[23]

Liberia had long been considered a ward of the United States since its settling by free African American emigrants and newly manumitted slaves in the nineteenth century. In response to growing fears among whites in the aftermath of the Gabriel Prosser insurrection, shifting racial demographics in the newly formed United States, and African American Paul Cuffe's successful transportation of thirty-eight free blacks to Sierra Leone, white statesmen, philanthropists, blackphobes, and religious leaders organized the American Colonization Society (ACS). The society's primary objective was the repatriation of free black Americans to their homeland of Africa.[24] The ship *Elizabeth* set sail for the west coast of Africa on February 6, 1820, with eighty-six free blacks and three white agents from the ACS. After great hardships—deaths due to malaria and wars with neighboring tribes—by 1824 the settlers had named the territory Liberia, an allusion to their newfound freedom, and its capital Monrovia, in honor of President James Monroe, a supporter of the colonization efforts.

After a succession of ACS-appointed white administrators to oversee the evolving nation-state and its continuing expansion through the usurpation of surrounding lands from indigenous Africans, Amero-Liberians achieved self-rule in 1842. But threats of encroachment as a result of British and French colonial expansion in Africa called the sovereignty of the Commonwealth of Liberia into question. Embroiled in its own political woes on the home front—abolitionist activity, slavery, and an impending civil war—the United States, looked to as a sort of mother country by the ex-colonists, effectively declared to the European colonial powers that Liberia was an independent state. Despite joint efforts by the ACS and the American government over the years, which filtered monies, supplies, and military protection against both European colonial powers and indigenous Africans, the United States offered no protection or support to the nascent independent nation-state.[25] Realizing the need to take their fate into their own hands, in 1847 twelve Liberian officials drew up a declaration of independence and a constitution, severing ties with the American Colonization Society. The opening lines of the Liberian Declaration of Independence echoed the American Declaration of Independence but continued on in important distinctions:

> We, the people of the Republic of Liberia, were originally the inhabitants of the United States of North America. . . .
>
> We were made a separate and distinct class, and against us every avenue to improvement was effectually closed. Strangers from all lands of a color different from ours were preferred before us.
>
> We uttered complaints, but they were unattended to, or met only by alleging the peculiar institution of the country.
>
> All hope of a favorable change in our country was thus wholly extinguished in our bosom, and we looked with anxiety abroad for some asylum from the deep degradation.

With the signing and ratification of the constitution and declaration, Liberia elected its first president in 1847, Joseph Jenkins Roberts, and was officially recognized as a nation by European powers. The United States, however, did not recognize the republic until the Civil War, when President Lincoln authorized the exchange of ambassadors.

Even though the country was the second black republic to declare its sovereignty officially, Liberia's challenges and economic dependence on the United States did not end. All peoples living in the republic were declared Liberians by 1904 under President Arthur Barclay, but divisions of color, class, and ethnicity emerged, with the propertied class, immigrant Amero-Liberians, and mixed-race Amero-Liberians enjoying privileges denied to the indigenous populations. Internecine color battles also surfaced between the mixed-race classes and "black" Amero-Liberians. Intermarriage between the natives and the founding immigrants, particularly between Amero-Liberian women and native men, was expressly frowned upon. Discrimination against the indigenous populations was rampant and reminiscent of the American system of segregation. By the time of the International Commission's visit, in 1930, twelve to fifteen thousand Amero-Liberians "presum[ed] to control an area of 43,000 square miles and an unknown native population of about 1.5 million."[26] Issues such as pawning, an indigenous practice whereby one might exchange a family member for a sum of money; forced native labor, particularly as it was tied to the American rubber corporation Firestone; and the various loans assured by the American government combined to yoke Liberia and America in a quasi-colonial relation. Moreover, the Liberian government called for American assistance to help quell a native rebellion in 1918. The issue of forced labor notably went counter to the League of Nations Antislavery Convention of 1926, which most European powers with interests in Africa signed but to which the United States remained noncommittal. Despite the peonage system in the American South, the forced labor of Mexicans in the Southwest, and the plantation system in Hawaii, the United States government maintained that slavery and other forms of forced labor on the continuum of slavery were a nonissue.[27] The Liberian situation presented a glaring contradiction in American policy within the theater of world politics.

The United States State Department (USSD), under pressures stemming from the allegations of slavery and other forms of forced labor in Liberia, assembled the International Commission in cooperation with the Republic of Liberia to investigate the situation. In 1930, three representatives were appointed by the Liberian government, the USSD, and the League of Nations—one from Liberia, former president Arthur Barclay; one from the United States, the African American Charles Johnson; and the British explorer and health researcher Cuthbert Christy. The results were outlined in the 207-page "Christy Commission" report, written ostensibly by Johnson although the report bears Christy's name. Johnson, a sociologist trained at the University of Chicago, was the author of the posthumously published volume *Bitter Canaan: The Story of the Negro Republic.* His reflections in the book were critical of Liberia, particularly around the native question. Discouraged from publishing the volume by members of the American black bourgeoisie who feared that "'airing such linen' publicly would confirm white notions regarding blacks[']" inability to govern themselves, Johnson put the volume aside.[28] The American black bourgeoisie, mostly of a Pan-Africanist persuasion, empathized with the Amero-Liberian elite and firmly believed, in the tradition of Alexander Crummell and Martin Delany, that Liberia's very existence as a black republic, as a symbol of freedom, black self-determination, superseded native rights. The indigenous populations were viewed either as "backward" and in need of Western education by some black American factions or as a hindrance to the republic's development.[29]

But Johnson's *Bitter Canaan* did offer some insight into the question of black American immigration to Liberia in the 1930s, which vacillated between an open-door policy that would introduce foreign capital and a focus on internal problems that would lead to a closed-door immigration policy.[30] Further, the race-conscious Pan-Africanist politics of black Americans were perceived by the Amero-Liberian elite as antagonistic to their own interests in keeping the goodwill of their American financial allies and European colonial neighbors. When *La Revue* editor Léo Sajous explained in 1931 that there had been no attempt to stem the tide of immigration, a somewhat misleading note resonated. According to Sajous, the drop in black American immigration was voluntary in nature:

> The emancipation of the American Negro, the subsequent constitutional amendment which accorded him the suffrage, and the opportunities for industrial, financial, and intellectual development which these two privileges opened up to him, were responsible for the drying up of the stream of immigration of the American Negro into Liberia.[31]

Sajous also reasoned that the American Negro, having fought for such rights, decided to continue the fight for total equality in the United States. By way of critique nonetheless, Sajous asserted that those "men" of intellect and industriousness who could benefit Liberia in its development were "so engrossed in stabilizing [their] undertakings that it is only with the greatest difficulty that [they have] realized that the problem of the emancipation of the Negro is universal" (13).

Interestingly, Sajous suggested that the American Negro's assiduousness in the pursuit of justice and parity at home cultivated a tunnel-visioned understanding of the "black problem" globally. Black Americans, with their "self-imposed isolation" (13), had hitherto run counter to the notion of "the great Brotherhood" that would transcend national boundaries outlined in *La Revue*'s "Our Aim." Sajous echoed the sentiments of Du Bois when, in his "Negro at Paris" exposé, he wrote of his attempts to collectivize and internationalize the Negro struggle in 1919 against "Negroes who may argue vociferously that the Negro problem is a domestic matter to be settled in Richmond and New Orleans."[32]

Du Bois's racial Pan-Africanism and anti-imperialism were nonetheless shunted aside by Sajous for Marcus Garvey's "torrential eloquence"[33] on race consciousness and black self-determination:

> On the contrary, the members of the United Negro Improvement Association and the African Communities Leagues are of an entirely different category. Under the leadership of Marcus Garvey, who assumed the title of President General of Africa, their openly avowed slogan is: "Africa for the Africans." They assert that every European government in Africa is an intruder, and furthermore that the millions of Negroes now in the United States should be transported to Africa, immediately given possession, and allowed to assume the direction of the entire continent. Briefly stated, the Liberian attitude endorses this policy.[34]

Sajous inserted immediately after this endorsement of Garveyism the objections raised by the Liberian nation-state to black Americans' taking over the country "en bloc" (13). Garvey had importantly singled out Liberia as a potential site for his provisional African government. In a counter-Garvey moment, Sajous further suggested that Liberia would never sow seeds of discord in neighboring African countries under the yoke of European colonialism: "Nor will Liberia permit her Negro brothers from the United States or elsewhere to use Liberian territory as a hotbed for fomenting dissatisfaction in the minds of the surrounding Africans who happen to be at present under the government of European powers" (13). In response to pressure from Liberia's European colonial neighbors, the republic's positions on Garveyism, race consciousness, Pan-Africanism, and black American immigration are here reiterated by Sajous. Yet this riposte came a little too late for French authorities, for the stamp of Garveyism, shored up by the founding editor despite the overwhelmingly Afro-Latin, New Negro thrust of *La Revue du monde noir,* remained. Moreover, the conclusion to Sajous's article, which called on Negro Americans to pay homage to Liberia as "the first Negro Republic" in Africa that did not rely upon the "standards of European culture" (14), struck a solidly political and antiassimilationist chord. The notion of "the first Negro Republic" naturally conjured up, in the French political unconscious, images of Haiti, the first black republic in the Caribbean, whose liberation was accompanied by the massacre of more than two million French citizens and the destruction of $1.5 million in property. But possibly more incriminating than this allusion from the viewpoint of the French authorities was that Léo Sajous held simultaneously an editorial position with *La Race nègre,* the organ for the Ligue de défense de race nègre. *La Race nègre* combined a subtle Garveyism with socialism from 1931 to 1932.[35]

In that same December 1931 issue of the *La Revue du monde noir,* E. Grégoire-Micheli's discerning essay "La Mentalité des Noirs est-elle inférieure?" appeared. As a member of the International Institute of Anthropology, Grégoire-Micheli was highly versed in eighteenth- and nineteenth-century anthropological theories on race and twentieth-century pseudoscientific doctrines on intelligence, inequality, and race. He opens his analysis by taking to task Gobineau's convoluted hierarchy of races and "specious theories concerning the formation of the skull" as it reflects "the psychological value" of individuals and their ancestors as well as their progeny.[36] "Are these methods scientific?" the anthropologist queries wryly. Whether scientifically valid or not, "every white nation has adjusted them to the needs of her own policy . . . [and] Negroes in particular have been and are still suffering from it" (20–21). The peculiarities of race prejudice, especially the absurd belief in racial superiority, have led to the creation of untenable doctrines to benefit the white race rather than the human race. Contrary to the lapses in scientific integrity demonstrated by his colleagues, Grégoire-Micheli is quite methodical in detailing the erroneous nature of "scientific" pronouncements on the psychology of the Negro, stereotyping, and black racial and cultural inferiority. In a somewhat eerie foreshadowing of the intelligence-quotient wars at the turn of the twenty-first century appearing in such runaway best-sellers as *The Bell Curve,*[37] he insists that "whatsoever might be the similarity of their physical characteristics, there are not two individuals who have the same psychological rating" (21). Broad-sweeping pronouncements on the collective intellectual inferiority of any racial group are simply pronouncements, and opinions, not science. Given the diversity among individual blacks within the same nation and the diversity of blacks dispersed globally in nations of varying stages of technological and economic advancement, psychological deviations would necessarily be serious. The "worthlessness" of the data amassed from the "representative" sample is "more obvious than

> that witticism of Tolstoi's, which the newspapers used to take such pleasure in recalling some time ago: "What have we in common with the French? They are sensualists; the spiritual nature is much less important to them than the flesh. For a Frenchman, woman is everything. They are a worn out people who no longer have vigor." "Italy is the country of quacks and adventurers; only Arétins, Casanovas, Cagliostras, and others of the like persuasion are born there." Is there not a striking analogy between these unreflected and therefore unjust sallies, and the hackneyed ideas uttered on the subject of Negroes? (22)

Drawing upon more progressive development theories on Africa, Grégoire-Micheli proceeds then in the vein of economic historians and dependency theorists to explore Africa's centuries-long geographic isolation as a primary factor in its stagnated economic and technological development in a capitalist-driven world order. Its diversity, vastness, and, more importantly, its inaccessibility foreclosed the dynamism that occurs with sociological crossbreeding. Were it not for Europe's accessibility for peoples migrating from "the Orient," he hypothesizes, the European continent would have similarly suffered such undevelopment. Grégoire-Micheli does not, however, explore the debilitating demographic impact of the transatlantic and trans-Saharan slave trades, the violent and retrogressive European incursions into the continent, or the deliberate center/periphery economic relationship between Africa and Europe that immensely contributes to African underdevelopment and dependency.

The anthropologist's explications resonate with the general thrust of *La Revue* on the dialectical nature of cross-cultural, racial, and sociological contacts as well as the questions raised in the debut issue's opening commentary by managing director Louis-Jean Finot, titled "Égalité des Races." "Let us smile at those misinformed individuals who talk of the French 'race,'" Finot writes. "France is indeed a superior nation and we are justly very proud of her, but we must admit that she is a product of a wide mixture of races, the living example of the result of a peaceful fusion of kindred spirits from different races which not only form the basis of her composition but change her aspect from one day to another."[38] Finot's emphasis on "peaceful fusion" in the history of France's development necessarily invokes a syncretic or synergizing activity that leads to something new. Smitten with the 1931 Colonial Exposition and its displays of African art, sculpture, and other cultural riches, and urging collaboration and *métissage, La Revue du monde noir* was culturally antipassive-assimilationist[39] and essentially colonially reformist. Hence, Finot could clamor, without seeming contradiction, for racial equality and a "collaborative" vision of Euro-Africa—one that Senghor would advocate in 1949—whereby Africa would stimulate the postwar European economy:

> One of the cures for the Depression, insomuch as France [is] concerned, would be to put to profitable use the African continent in the capacity of a huge colonial market. Let us add, not only for France but for the whole of Europe. . . . Out of the community of interests . . . will come a fruitful cooperation which will bring together Europe and Africa, and will prove to be one of the cures for the economic crisis.[40]

Finot's and Grégoire-Micheli's essays work hand in glove. Finot's editorial sounds a call for the end to race prejudice and the debunking of myths of black racial inferiority in order to form a more perfect racial and economic union between Africa and Europe, and the anthropologist's provides a more methodical study of those specious myths of inferiority which would prevent such a union from coming into existence.

From his anthropological arsenal, Grégoire-Micheli deploys an extensive citation on African civilizations by ethnologist Maurice Delafosse. Former governor of the colonies and professor at the École coloniale and the École des langues orientales vivantes at Paris, Delafosse wrote *Les Noirs de l'Afrique* (1921), *Civilisations nègro-africaines* (1925) and *Les Nègres* (1927)—extensive studies on the languages, cultural traditions, and histories of French Equatorial Africa. Delafosse writes:

> The Negroes of Africa present a spectacle unmatched the world over of a race forced to rely wholly upon itself for development, having received nothing from the outside world, or having been the object of as many,

if not more, thrusts in the direction of retrogression, than that of progress. . . . When people placed in such conditions have been able, depending upon their resources alone, to organize States; to establish and maintain study centers such as, for example Timbuctu *[sic]*; to produce statesmen like the "mansa" Gongo-Moussa or the "askia" Mohammed, . . . scientists and writers, who, without the aid of dictionaries or of recourse to any translation, have succeeded in mastering Arabic, . . . and more recently the Bamoun of Cameroun, a system of writing which is likely to endure, it must be admitted that these people do not deserve being treated as inferiors from the intellectual point of view.[41]

In one citation, Grégoire-Micheli attempts to put to rest theories of African intellectual inferiority based on the geographic isolationist model of African economic stagnation. Isolation did not dull the faculties of Africans; rather, it effectively left them vulnerable in the area of technological modernization. To the charge of African atavism, Grégoire-Micheli catalogs European and/or white atavistic tendencies, namely the "incomprehensible" U.S. lynch law and "the vendetta and banditry of Corsica."[42] Notwithstanding the relatively new freed status of blacks in both the New World and the old colonies of France—less than one hundred years in the British colonies, eighty-three years in the French colonies, and sixty-eight years in the United States in 1931— and unequal access to education, the anthropologist provides "a very brief summary" of "the immense progress" of the African diaspora (24). Borrowing from the essentializing thesis articulated in *Revue* editor Clara Shepard's 1932 article "Les Noirs Américains et les langues étrangères,"[43] Grégoire-Micheli maintains that Negroes possess a "great facility . . . in learning foreign languages."[44] Turning again toward Delafosse on the vibrancy of African art, followed by a gesture toward the literary and musical contributions of black Americans to American culture, Grégoire-Micheli concludes his contribution to *La Revue du monde noir* much in the same way as René Maran concludes *Un homme pareil aux autres*: "A Negro is a man like any other" (27).

4. Paulette Nardal: Antillean Literature and Race Consciousness

In the sixth and final issue of *La Revue du monde noir*, in April 1932, Paulette Nardal published a comparative historico-literary essay, "L'Éveil de la conscience de race chez les étudiants noirs," that not only broached the subject of colonialism and its effect on the evolution of modern Antillean writing but implored students and aspiring writers to engage with the "riches that the past of the black race and the African continent offers them."[1] Borrowing language from her sister Jane's 1928 essay "Internationalisme noir" (discussed in chapter 2), Paulette Nardal mapped out diasporic blacks' coming into consciousness and their articulation of an authentic self-consciousness in literature through three paradigmatic phases. By the essay's conclusion, she called for the awakening of race consciousness among cultural workers and intellectuals, and hence a displacement of Frenchness as the embodiment of culture and civilization. She explicitly linked race and the experiences of racialized subjects to cultural expressivity.

In the opening sentence of the six-page "Éveil de la conscience de race," Nardal asserts that she is concerned with this awakening among Antilleans in particular. Witnessing a modification in attitudes toward race and racial problems among the younger and older generations of Antilleans in the 1930s, Nardal writes: "A mere few years ago, one might even say a few months, certain subjects were taboo in Martinique. Woe to those who dared broach them! One could not speak of slavery nor proclaim pride in being of African descent without being considered a fanatic or at the very least eccentric" (25). What brought on this marked transformation in the Antillean Negro's consciousness? Through a literary historiography, Nardal proceeds to outline this evolution. Race con-

sciousness among a number of Antilleans was stirred in the late nineteenth century. This racial stirring was initially brought on when natives
left the colony for France. Exile and feelings of nonbelonging, or,
as Nardal writes, "uprooting and ensuing estrangement," provoked a
sensation of difference, often a malaise. The Antilleans for the first
time were forced to live their blackness and experience their difference,
their "Negro soul," despite their "Latin education" (25). However, the
Antillean Negroes never explicitly articulated this conflict, and French
liberalism and the policy of assimilation helped to mask French racialism. Thoroughly immersed in the history and culture of "nos ancestres
les Gaulois," the Antilleans would have found an identity invested in
denigrated and marginalized blackness quite simply untenable in the
their psyche. Nardal writes at length on the subject:

> The Antillean Negro's attitude regarding race, so different from that of
> black Americans, can easily be explained by the liberalism that char-
> acterizes French race politics vis-à-vis peoples of color. [Friedrich]
> Sieburg's book *Dieu est-il français?* contains, among other things, a very
> judicious observation on the assimilative force of the French spirit.
> According to the German writer, the absence of color prejudice among
> the French is owing to their certainty of turning the Negro, in a rela-
> tively short time, into a true Frenchman. Besides, it is natural that Antil-
> leans, products of race mixing, black and white, imbued with Latin cul-
> ture, and ignorant of the history of the black race, should in the end
> turn toward the element that honors them the most. (26)

Nardal characterizes the French attitude toward "people of color"
varyingly in the space of a paragraph as "liberal" and "absent of color
prejudice" based on the surety of the assimilation to the universal that,
as Jules Michelet observed, is Frenchness.[2] The inevitability of becoming French coupled with the racial admixture of Antilleans and their ig-
norance of black history—trumped by the acculturating nature of the
French education system, where educational institutions existed—leads
to the identification on the part of Antilleans with France, and with
Frenchness rather than blackness. And who could or would resist becoming French, thus becoming, as the French believed, part of the civilized human community? Race and racial problems were not especially
pressing, at least from the standpoint of the Antilleans. There was no
need to search for an identity outside of the universal French identity

that had been bestowed upon them. Conversely, racially mixed American Negroes confronted issues of race, racial identity, and difference daily. As Nardal notes,

> The systematic scorn displayed by white America toward them inspired them to look for reasons, from a historical, cultural, and social point of view, for pride in the past of the black race. Consequently, race, because of the necessity to resolve the racial problem plaguing the United States since the abolition of slavery, became the core of their concerns. (26)

Nardal then compares and contrasts the development of race-conscious literature among African Americans to that of Antilleans. "As is the case with nearly all colonized people," she writes, "three characteristic periods may be noted in the intellectual evolution of black Americans" (26). Because of the persistence and virulence of American racism, African American writers consistently had been the subject of and had been subjected to the "race problem"—thus their identity as black. African Americans, like Antilleans, passed through the Nardalian imitative phase because of their initial uprooting and forced immersion into a foreign and hostile environment; their creative expressions were necessarily imitative: "This is a period of Negro absorption. . . . Only certain slave narratives retain all of their original freshness and genuine emotion thanks to the use of the African-American dialect" (26). Here the parallels between Nardal's essay and Alain Locke's essay "The New Negro" are uncanny. The "phases" paradigm of black race consciousness outlined in Locke's book *The New Negro* and adopted by Jane Nardal in "Internationalisme noir" is also present in "L'Éveil de la conscience de race" in mutated forms. Paulette Nardal uses the term *imitative* to characterize the first phase, whereas Locke describes the first phase of his "progressive phases" of Negro consciousness as "a sort of protective social mimicry forced upon him [the Negro] by the adverse circumstances of dependence" and a "psychology of imitation and implied inferiority."[3]

Nardal offers no examples of imitative literature or slave narratives written in dialect by black Americans. Interestingly, even the earliest emancipatory slave narratives written in English by African Americans such as Briton Hammon and the African Olaudah Equiano were intentionally quite polished. Nardal may be referring to recorded oral histories, testimonies, folk spirituals, and antebellum slave songs like "Wade in Nah Watah, Childun" and "Raise a Ruckus Tonight" rather than the propagandistic antislavery narratives that most often were accompanied by the phrase "written by himself [or herself]" as proof of black genuis even under the duress of slavery and laws prohibiting their education.

African American writers next pass through Nardal's second phase: "a literature of controversy and moral protest" amid antislavery agitation.[4] Various fictional memoirs, such as Harriet Wilson's *Our Nig, or Sketches from the Life of a Free Black* (1859), and slave narratives, such as Harriet Jacobs's powerful *Incidents in the Life of a Slave Girl* (1861), Sojourner Truth's *Narrative* (1850), and Frederick Douglass's classic *Narrative* (1845), which, for Nardal, attempt to appeal to a sense of morality, pity, and moral indignation, necessarily characterize this stage of African American letters. Although race was a "core" theme in these writings as a result of its use in constricting the lives of the writers, African American literature at this stage was not, for Nardal, a literature racialized in the defense or glorification of the Negro race, but a literature intended to appeal to the morality and ethics of whites regarding the inhumanity of slavery.

From 1880 onward, African American writers entered into a period when they ascended to, in Nardal's words, "true culture."[5] Through W. E. B. Du Bois's social-protest literature, Paul Laurence Dunbar's "school of racial realism," and the poetry of Claude McKay and Langston Hughes, reprinted in the pages of the review, Nardal insists that one can "observe that the Americans, having thrown off all inferiority complexes, tranquilly "express their individual dark-skinned selves without fear or shame."[6]

A race literature imbued with a feminine-gendered particularity is missing from Nardal's analyses of the African American literary tradition. The writers she does mention—Hughes, Du Bois, McKay, Cullen—are male Negro Renaissance writers.[7] This erasure, somewhat inexplicable given the inclusion of women writers in *The New Negro,* may be due to Nardal's limited encounters, through formal education as well as in the Clamart and Maran salons in Paris, with Negro Renaissance women writers. Harriet Beecher Stowe's *Uncle Tom's Cabin* was in fact her introduction to African American life.

Antillean writers' broaching of racial themes in literature developed less rapidly than African Americans'. Antilleans seemed content to immerse themselves more deeply in the culture of the *métropole* in order to avoid confronting this consciousness; the writers were content to imitate rather than create for fear of giving life to this difference through their art. Creativity would force them to confront their situation. Antillean writers seesawed between the imitative phase and the literature of controversy and moral protest regarding colonial reforms. Nardal attributes this slower awakening, again, to the cultural and historical differences between French and American race politics and intraracial island antagonisms. If American blacks were battling for equal rights with whites after emancipation, the lack of "racial concerns . . . in the literary productions of the period following the abolition of slavery in the Antilles . . . [was] because our 'Great Forefathers' were busy struggling for liberty and political rights for the various categories of the black race on Antillean soil."[8] As a member of the black bourgeoisie whose civil-servant father suffered discrimination at the hands of the French government, Nardal was keenly aware of the racial caste system—divided into *mulâtre, nègre,* and métis, among other racial designations—that existed in the French West Indies and, importantly, was created and stoked by the *métropole.* Her father, according to Eslanda Goode Robeson, served "more than sixteen years" as the manager of the Department of Highways and Bridges. Despite his honorably retiring from the position, the colonial administration "never formally recognized his position," believing that his "being a pure Negro" meant that it was "bad policy for him to hold such a position."[9] In the interview "Black Paris," Robeson writes that Nardal believed that "had he been mulatto, the Government would probably have [officially] appointed him" (9). Robeson continues her summation of Nardal's position on the racial caste system in Martinique:

> This question of mulattoes is a most unfortunate one; the white people feel much less prejudice against them and in consequence they usually secure the best positions in the Civil Services. They have quite a different psychology, too: they are primarily interested in becoming white, and in being assimilated. The pure Negroes are very proud, and resentful of this. (9)

The tensions between the privileged "mulatto" class and the privileged black bourgeoisie are laid bare in Nardal's interview. The former class functioned as powerbrokers and buffers in the French West Indies. The racial divide also led to class fissures among blacks. Hence, as Nardal writes, Antilleans had to deal with internal race and class strife upon the abolition of slavery. In the United States, conversely, the "one-drop rule" with respect to racial mixing—that is, one drop of black blood rendered one black—and the dangerous mulatto stereotype bolstered by the success of D. W. Griffith's racially retrograde film *Birth of a Nation* foreclosed the formation of a powerful, buffering mixed-race elite. Passing was an issue; one need only read Nella Larsen's *Passing* and James Weldon Johnson's *Autobiography of an Ex-colored Man*. However, those interracial persons unable or unwilling to pass simply cast their political lot with the racially marked American "Negro."

Great Antillean writers, such as Daniel Thaly and Oruno Lara, were nonetheless present in the Antillean postemancipation era. Moreover, Nardal writes by way of consolation that "the productions of the Antillean writers were in no way inferior to those of French writers, not to mention such Antillean geniuses like the father and son Dumas."[10] The ideals of the French republic effectively obfuscated the very real issues of domination and its attendant results in the area of culture: alienation and false self-consciousness. Until 1914 Antillean writers were consistently and consciously imitative, lapsing into the standard forms of exoticism practiced by European writers as they wrote "lovingly of their native islands" (28). For Nardal, no race pride can be found in this literature; European travel writers, and even writers whose imagination traveled for them, feted the islands with more "appreciation" and "attachment" than the indigenous poets and writers did (28). Ever diplomatic and measured, Nardal levels a veiled critique at the West Indian literary bourgeoisie. Their literary creations had been hitherto unimaginative, uninspired, and uninspiring—"in no way inferior to those of French writers," but certainly not distinguishable. Taking his cue from Nardal, poet Étienne Léro would caustically write "Misère d'une poésie" in the June 1932 Marxist-surrealist *Légitime défense,* just two months after Nardal's review ceased publication, in April 1932:

> The West Indian writer, crammed to splitting open with white morality, white culture, white education, white prejudices, flaunts in his little books a puffed up image of himself. To be a good imitation of the white man satisfies both his social and his poetic needs. . . . "You are acting like a nigger," he does not fail to inveigh, if, in his presence, you cede to a natural exuberance. As well he does not want to "act like a nigger" in his poems. It is a point of honor with him that a white person could

read his entire book without guessing his color. . . . The stranger will search in vain in this literature for an original or profound accent, the sensual and vivid imagination of the black. . . . An overdose of French esprit and classical humanities has brought us these chatterboxes and the soporific water of their poetry.[11]

Léro, like Nardal, offers up the creations of the Guadeloupean Oruno Lara and the Martinicans Daniel Thaly and Victor Duquesnay as examples of this "soporific" poetry. He mentions also, quite curiously, the "bric-brac of the last 150 years" of Gilbert Gratiant, contributor to the 1935 *L'Étudiant noir* (11).

Nardal writes that the period between the phase of conscious imitation of the literature of the metropolis by West Indian writers and the present—in effect, the interwar period—"may be classed a generation of men whose racial leanings are being channeled through literature or political and humanitarian concerns."[12] The "theories of Marcus Garvey" and the organization of the "first Pan-Negro Congress" influenced such concerns. René Maran and Kojo Tovalou's short-lived *Les Continents,* Maurice Satineau's *La Dépêche africaine,* and studies on the history of Guadeloupe emerged; and within Maran's preface to *Batouala* "a generous indignation stirs" (28). Nardal provides essentially an ideological genealogy of the development of *La Revue du monde noir.* It was particularly through the newspaper *La Dépêche africaine,* which embodied a hodgepodge of the aforementioned ideologies, that "the aspirations that were to crystallize around *La Revue du monde noir* asserted themselves" (29). With the connections between Garvey, Satineau, the colonial reformist Maran, and the "dangerously internationalist" politics of Du Bois confirmed in Nardal's historiographic literary essay, the Colonial Ministry withheld further funding for the review.

The emergent racial concerns in Paris did venture into the French Antilles, however:

> In the Antilles, it is important to note the remarkable works of Jules Monnerot—*Contributions à l'historie de la Martinique*—and more recently *Les Galeries martiniquaises,* a valuable document that the author, Césaire Philémon, dedicated to his small homeland, and in which matters of race are treated with more frankness than usual.
>
> In none of these works is the black question studied in itself, as we can plainly attest. These works remain still the tributaries of Latin cul-

ture. In none of them is expressed faith in the future of the race and the necessity to create a feeling of solidarity between the different groups of blacks disseminated throughout the globe. (29)

Antillean writers still avoided racial subjects. Objective observation, rather than reflective subjectivizing narratives, dominated their writerly endeavors. Race continued to be a thorny issue for writers who were still more interested in expressing their facility with the French language and their grasp of literary aesthetics—critical in demonstrating that they were *French*. The idea that there was a future in blackness, a "future of the race," and that there was a particular lived experience of blackness that could somehow inspire feelings of transracial solidarity and a race literature was beyond the comprehension of Antillean writers. Race might exist, blackness might exist, but it was not accorded a crucial role in the formation of an Antillean identity or a grand place in the scheme of Antillean letters.

Nardal next moves on to a discussion of the veritable awakening of race consciousness among Antilleans. Parallel to the aforementioned string of developments and commentaries, indicative of some stirring of consciousness within Antilleans, was the desire to secure the future of the race in the annals of Franco-Antillean cultural history and the need for race solidarity among a group of Antillean women students:

> [T]he aspirations that were to crystallize around *La Revue du monde noir* asserted themselves among a group of Antillean women students in Paris. The women of color living alone in the metropolis, who until the Colonial Exposition were less favored than their male compatriots, who have enjoyed easy successes, felt long before the latter the need for a racial solidarity that would not be merely material. They were thus aroused to race consciousness. The feeling of uprooting, felicitously expressed in Roberte Horth's "Histoire sans importance," published in the second issue of *La Revue du monde noir* was the starting point of their evolution. (29)

In this passage, Nardal asserts clearly that Antillean women were at the vanguard of the racialized cultural revolution that would later be called Negritude and identified as male-inspired and -forged. It was the women who recognized a need for racial solidarity, who had first experienced a veritable race consciousness; it was the women who, "[a]fter having been trained obediently in the school of thought of their white models . . . perhaps passed, like their black American brothers, through a period of revolt" to their "present position" on the "middle ground" (29). Nardal cites Roberte Horth's short story "Histoire sans importance" as capturing quintessentially the experiences of black women in Paris. Horth's story explores the feelings of Léa, a young Antillean woman who leaves "a little cottage with green blinds, on some wild windswept shore," to be steeped in "Western literature and disciplined by different methods of thinking" at the lycée and the university in France.[13] In three different moments in the story, Horth uses variations of the phrase "just like any other" when referring to Léa, only then to highlight the ways in which her differences are constantly thrown into relief. Her name, Léa, is, for Horth, "just a name like any other, common and short, without any meaning unless implied by mother love"; she is "just a child like the others" and, later, "like any other young woman born of the cultured and refined people of whom she felt herself a part" (50). But at each instance, Léa's difference is raised by her white French compatriots, whether through being exotically renamed by "her friends and comrades . . . with some queer nickname full of aroma of strange fruits, of unknown fragrance, of weird dances and far-off lands" (48) or through being excluded from "the intimacy of their homes" (50). Léa is treated as an interesting but marginal "fetish," a "doll to be proudly exhibited" but not held (50). The Antillean woman in Paris, learned in the ways of occidental culture yet rejected by that culture on the basis of her ethnicity, gender, and color, experiences a profound social isolation. Such isolation gives way to an understanding of certain racial and racist realities in the metropolis, to a crisis in identity that is productively transformed into a desire to create a community and a new identity. She is not a Frenchwoman like other Frenchwomen; she is a racialized Franco-Antillean woman.

This realization echoes, importantly, novelist Mayotte Capécia's award-winning *Je suis Martiniquaise* (1948), in which the protagonist maintains pitifully, "Je suis Française tout comme aut" [I am a Frenchwoman like any other], only to be told by a colonial administrator that she is "forget[ting] that you are a woman of color."[14] Horth concludes "Histoire sans importance" just as abysmally:

> In this country, she will never be a woman like the others, with a right to a woman's happiness, because she will never be able to blot out, for the others, the absurdity of her soul fashioned by occidental culture but

concealed by an objectionable skin. She sighed; she had only overlooked one little fact, a thing of no importance, the simple irony of her mixed blood.[15]

It is ultimately Léa's exclusion as a "woman of color" that creates her unhappiness. Race may be a thing of no importance superficially; but, as Horth demonstrates, the "one little fact" of Léa's mixed blood is of utter importance. And it is her discovery of its importance that sets the stage for a racially gendered consciousness. Using Horth's narrative of "uprooting" and alienation as a point of reference, Nardal's essay also reveals itself as an official record of black Francophone Antillean women's collective critical conscious. Nardal's last contribution to *La Revue du monde noir*, in effect, stands as a corrective to modern and postmodern male-centered narratives on the evolution of black Francophone literature and race consciousness.

Nardal again elaborated upon the black feminine dimensions of this newly found and celebrated race consciousness among French-speaking black intellectuals in the 1930s four years later, in the June 1936 interview-essay "Black Paris," with Eslanda Goode Robeson. In her chronicling of the evolution of race consciousness among women, Nardal describes the curious situation of black male privilege and black female circumscription in matters of race, sex, and class. Unlike their black and mixed-race male counterparts in France, who successfully threw themselves, as Nardal remarks, into the pursuit of French women, educated women of color were isolated, ignored by fellow Antilleans and unable to be fully accepted into French culture and by French men other than on certain defined interracial terms.[16] Being again the ever-cultured woman, Nardal uses the word *friend* in her interview with Robeson to describe the parameter of French male–Antillean female relationships; but she further states that many of the French women pursued by men of color were from a lower socioeconomic class and that on the island those liaisons would have been frowned upon. Educated Antillean women, much more sensitive to issues of class, according to Nardal, were less willing to interact with white men who were not of their class, and race prevented many educated French men from interacting with serious intentions with Antillean women. Here again we turn to the instructive experiences of writer Mayotte Capécia's protagonist. At the conclusion of *Je suis Martiniquaise,* she expresses this same sentiment with respect to interracial relationships with Frenchmen: "I should have liked to be married, but to a white man. But a woman of color is never altogether respectable in a white man's eyes no matter how much he loves her. I knew that."[17]

Antillean women's desire for a community in Paris, their "uprooting," Nardal continues, had been "the starting point of their evolution." While the literary men of the era for the most part sidestepped their responsibilities to become racially engaged writers and a number of Antillean male students partook of the fruit of (sexual) French liberalism in full swing, these young race women threw themselves into the study of the black race and on their respective countries, and began lamenting the impoverished curricula on the subject of "the race" in Antillean schools.[18] The women students wrote papers and theses on the Antilles and Antillean writers. In an autobiographical moment, Nardal mentions one student who wrote her *diplôme d'études supérieures d'anglais* on Harriet Beecher Stowe's *Uncle Tom's Cabin*—coincidentally the very subject of Nardal's own *diplôme*. "We must say," Nardal begins in another surreptitious criticism of the French higher-education curriculum and its white, Western, hegemonic focus, "that at that time, Afro-American writers were completely unknown in France. . . . We have been informed that many students of English are preparing papers on Afro-American writers hitherto neglected, in spite of their evident value, in the surveys of American literature compiled by French university professors" (30).

What began as a descriptive essay, tracing the evolution of racial themes in the writings of the African diaspora, concludes with earnest prodding on the continued need for academic, literary, scientific, and artistic engagements with questions of race. As if reading the minds and copious notes of French government agents, Nardal asks, "Should one see in the tendencies here expressed an implicit declaration of war upon Latin culture and the white world in general?" Certainly not, she informs her readers. Without French culture, "we would have never become conscious of who we really are. But we want to go beyond this culture in order to give to our brethren . . . the pride of belonging to a race whose civilization is perhaps the oldest in the world" (31). Nardal suggests optimistically that some Antillean writers are on the brink of entering into "the last phase" of the evolution, the acquisition of "true culture" as noted in African American letters, and that *La Revue du monde noir* fully intends to publish these writers. The review was not allowed to fulfill its promise.

Paulette Nardal's prophetic last essay ushered in a stream of writing by Antillean and African students. In an atmosphere of French metropolitan racism, a "Negro" identity had been foisted upon Antilleans and Africans. This imposition was doubly shocking for the Antillean, who, according to Frantz Fanon, believed that "[t]he West Indian was not a Negro; he was a West Indian, that is to say a quasi-metropolitan. By this attitude the white justified the West Indian in his contempt for the African. The Negro, in short, was a man who inhabited Africa."[19] Nardal refers interestingly and with condescension to the masses of Antilleans as "attardés" [backward] "brothers" and "compatriots" twice in the essay and to the role of the race-conscious Antillean in lending a "helping hand" in the masses' Negro-identified evolution.[20] Although the essay is riddled with class elitism, in accepting a Negro identity and in proclaiming an "âme nègre" Nardal effectively encouraged Antilleans to accept their being in the world as blacks. In heeding her call, three students whose names would be forever associated with Negritude changed their courses of study: the nineteen-year-old Aimé Césaire began to write on the theme of the South in African American literature; Léon Damas examined African survivals in the West Indies; and Léopold Senghor, who had been writing on Baudelaire, began to study African ethnography and languages.[21] And among the women she undoubtedly influenced was a Martinican student named Suzanne Roussy.

5. Suzanne Césaire: *Tropiques,* Negritude, Surrealism, 1941–1945

Born in 1913 in Trois-Ilets, Martinique, the picturesque village where Napoleon's Joséphine also passed her adolescence, Suzanne Roussy was a philosophy student in Paris in the 1930s. As a member of the Association des étudiants martinquais en France, she too became interested in issues of identity, colonialism, alienation, assimilation, and black consciousness debated among French-speaking black students, writers, and intellectuals and eventually articulated in the pages of the organization's one-issue journal, *L'Étudiant noir.* Like Léon-Gontran Damas, Roussy did not publish in *L'Étudiant noir* but mingled with the crowd at the Clamart salon and read *La Revue du monde noir.* Her literary debut did not occur until the onset of the Second World War. In 1937, Suzanne Roussy became Suzanne Roussy Césaire. She returned with Aimé Césaire to their native land of Martinique in 1939, where she assumed a teaching position at the Lycée Victor Schoelcher. Among the lycée's students were the future global theorist of oppression Frantz Fanon and the creator of the concept of Antillanité, Edouard Glissant. Also on the teaching faculty was philosopher René Ménil, a contributor to the Marxist-surrealist pamphlet *Légitime défense.*

The mounting discontent of the French right during the 1930s—expressed most fervently in their cri de coeur "La France aux Français" [France for the French]—Germany's rapid rebuilding in the *après-guerre* years, and the attendant rise of fascism in Italy, Spain, and Germany would have grave consequences for France and Martinique. By June 1940, France, under the leadership of Marshal Henri Philippe Pétain, hero of Verdun in World War I, signed an armistice with Germany. Under the terms of the armistice, France was arbitrarily partitioned and occupied by Germany and paid a daily indemnity of Fr 400 million. Toppling the Third Republic and thereby ridding a sinful France of its perceived excesses, a right-wing, Nazi-collaborating *état français* at Vichy with Pétain at its helm administered France and its colonies. Names like Pétain and Admiral Robert would be forever associated with the Axis powers and Hitlerism. Under Pétain's Vichy government, there was very little cover for organizing among progressive cultural and political dissidents. The label of "Communist" was hurled at liberals and other leftists with frequency and swiftness. Suzanne Roussy, who frequently skipped the school's morning *la Marseillaise* ritual in protest of the tyrannical and racist nature of the state, was repeatedly threatened with dismissal from the faculty.[1] The democratic principles of liberty, equality, and fraternity that were held as sacrosanct in France were quickly dispensed with during the Nazi collaboration era of 1940–1944. A repressive intellectual climate reigned on the island of Martinique under Admiral Robert and in France proper. Freedoms of the press were stamped out in favor of censorship; and groups and individuals committed to human freedom and transformation were routinely persecuted, imprisoned, or exiled.

Inspired after his initial return to his homeland in 1937, while still a student in Paris, Aimé Césaire published *Cahier d'un retour au pays natal* in 1939 in *Volontés* with no literary fanfare. The work encapsulated the discontent of the race-conscious, metropolitan-educated black intelligentsia returning en masse to Martinique at the dawning of the war. The rose-tinted glasses, as the cliché goes, were removed, and the horrendous facts of Martinican existence were poetically laid bare. The island of Martinique and its people, mired in dire poverty because of colonialism and choking on bilious stereotypes of intellectual and cultural inferiority, continued to look toward France as the model of cultural excellence—one to be appropriated and imitated. Criticisms of West Indian literature as imitative, servile, sterile, and inauthentic began in April 1932, with Paulette Nardal's essay "L'Éveil de la conscience de race chez les étudiants noirs," only to be quickly followed up, in June 1932, with the publication of *Légitime défense*. Within this manifesto's pages, Étienne Léro and René Ménil challenged their West Indian literary forebears and contemporaries to create an original literature. Primarily taken to task were such notables as the Guadeloupean Emmanuel Flavia-Léopold and the Martinican Gilbert Gratiant on the basis of their perceived pedantic poetic mediocrity and their strict adherence to the romantic and French Parnassian schools of poetry. As Ménil writes in "Généralités sur 'l'écrivain' de couleur antillais":

> [T]he Antillean of color makes the tour of ideas (broadminded, he says) and finds himself among the last who appreciate the artificial character of the infatuation with Greco-Roman bric-a-brac, the Parthenon. . . . *This abstract and objectively hypocritical literature interests no one: not the white because it is only a poor imitation of French literature of yesteryears; nor the black for the same reason.* . . . Boredom, condemnation of the self by the self, weighs upon the shoulders of the black Caribbean writer. His works are bored and boring; depressed, depressing.[2]

Less the sardonic tone, Ménil's commentary echoes that of Nardal's. At the heart of Ménil's polemic is an analysis of the depersonalization inherent in West Indian writers' prose and poetic verse. Black Caribbean writers were so thoroughly alienated and enamored with Francocentric cultural practices, thus suppressing passions and emotions that could be construed as outside of that tradition, that they were blinded to "the feeling of the cane cutter before the implacable factory, the feeling of solitude experienced by blacks throughout the world, the revolt against injustices in which [the Antillean] suffers above all in his own country, the love of love, the love of alcohol dreams, the love of inspired dances."[3] The genius of New "American" Negro writers, whose focus on the folk and folklore seemed to convey a sense of originality, is also cited as inspiration for their Francophone counterparts. Committed to recreating this dynamism in Martinican literature and culture, Suzanne Césaire, Aimé Césaire, and René Ménil founded the cultural review *Tropiques*.

In the review's fourth issue, in January 1942, Suzanne Césaire offered her own critique of West Indian literature in "Misère d'une poésie: John Antoine-Nau":

> Talent? Certainly for those that it interests. But what a pity! He [the West Indian writer] looks. But he has not "seen." [H]e does not know the Negro soul. . . . It is graceful. It is overdone. Literature? Yes. Literature of the hammock. Sugar and vanilla literature. Literary tourism. Blue Guide and C. G. T. Poetry, not so. . . . [T]rue poetry is elsewhere. . . . Martinican poetry will be cannibal or it will not be.[4]

In her use of the word *cannibal,* Césaire issues a literary decree regarding the orientation and even existence of Martinican poetry, plotting conceptually the course of an original West Indian literature. The Martinican writer would assimilate, cannibalize, and appropriate white, Western culture, its various theoretical tools, and its language in the exploration and articulation of the specificities of Martinican experiences and reality. Certainly Césaire's ideas reflect the currency and continuity of thought espoused by early Negritude women writers like the *soeurs* Nardal. In this new cannibalizing mode, the writers of *Tropiques,* more specifically both Césaires, adopted as their critical and artistic tool of choice a Negritude inflected with surrealism—a poetic movement steeped in Hegelian dialectics and Freudian psychoanalysis and equally committed to human freedom. For her part, Suzanne Césaire's use of surrealism allowed her to push the envelope of Negritude's Africanist parameters as espoused by Aimé Césaire, to include the specificity of the Martinican situation. She theorized a Negritude that recognized the racial and cultural *métissage* of the island, its history of "le brassage le plus continu" [the most continuous brazing] as she writes in "Malaise d'une civilisation."[5] Africa has its place in the Martinique sun, but, as she writes in "1943: Le Surréalisme et nous," the time has come to "transcend finally the sordid antinomies of today: whites-blacks, Europeans-Africans, civilized-savages."[6] "[D]elivering the bread of its depth" (18), Suzanne Césaire's Negritude set in motion the idea of the plurality of Martinican origins as a result of historical processes, a Negritude that would definitely offer intellectual sustenance to the hybridizing theories of Antillanité and Creolité.

SURREALISM AND THE RACE-CONSCIOUS MARTINICAN

Referred to the as "the pope of surrealism," French poet André Breton was the movement's principal founder, in 1924, with his *Manifeste du surréalisme.* Breton followed up the first volume with the *Second manifeste du surréalisme* in 1930. The affinity between Martinican race radicals and Bréton's surrealism was a natural one. As a matter of course, Ménil, in *Légitime défense* (which was named after a September 1926 surrealist treatise by Breton of the same title), clearly declared in the pamphlet's 1932 "Déclaration" that the destiny of Antilleans was tied to surrealism.[7] This "Déclaration" went on to suggest readings of Breton's surrealist manifestos and works by Paul Éluard and René Crevel, among other members of the Surrealist Group.[8] On an artistic level, surrealism rejected aesthetics, moral concerns, and literary and artistic values as elitist, repressive, and requiring conformity. Such values and ideas about technique clashed with the surrealist credo of calling into question "reality"—which was seen as essentially rooted in exploitation and inequality—with the hope of creating a "superior reality," a *sur-réalité*. "Automatic writing," a writing unrestrained by controlled thought (the ego), a writing from the Freudian unconscious (the id), offered the opportunity for free association rather than staid secondhand ideas and binary oppositions; it allowed for the exploration of the many layers of an inner reality and its relationship with the external world. In writing about surrealism and the automatic-writing process, Breton notes, "[P]sychic automatism in its pure state [is that] by which one proposes to express—verbally, by means of the written word, or in any other manner—the actual functioning of thought. Dictated by thought, in the absence of any control exercised by reason, exempt from any aesthetic and moral concern."[9] Surrealism opened horizons rather than closed them. As Breton continues in his "once and for all definition" of surrealism: "Surrealism is based on the belief in the superior reality of certain forms of previously neglected associations, in the omnipotence of dreams, in the disinterested play of thought. It tends to ruin once and for all all other psychic mechanisms and to substitute itself for them in solving all the principal problems of life" (26). The mind was to be freed of rationalism, logic, reason, and Cartesian philosophy, the supposed cornerstones of Western bourgeois culture and ideology, which occasioned autocensorship and repression of basic drives. Poetry and plastic arts were the vehicles through which a superior reality could be actualized. Tapping into the unconscious revealed one's desires, one's most primal and primitive instincts and conflicts. By writing, drawing, or painting that inner world, poets and artists served revolutionary ends—interpreting that world through words and craft and thereby revealing or demasking such poetics to the world at large and to their communities in particular.

For the Martinican New Negroes, who decried the unraced subject matter, the suppression of issues of identity, race, and culture, as well as the "flunkeyism," in Aimé Césaire's words, of Caribbean writers of color "of old," surrealism affirmed and converged with their agenda. The Surrealist Group's 1931 challenge to the Colonial Exposition in its

"Murderous Humanitarianism" tract (a critique of imperialism and racism), its internationalist reach, and its identification with working-class causes rooted in Hegelian and Marxian dialectical materialism and philosophies of liberation aligned the group politically with the antiracist and class-conscious writers and theoreticians of *Tropiques*. As Breton remarked in an interview with René Bélance:

> Surrealism is allied with peoples of colour, first because it has always taken their side against all forms of imperialism and white banditry . . . and secondly because of the profound affinities that exist between surrealism and so-called "primitive" thought, both of which seek the abolition of the conscious and the everyday, leading to the conquest of revelatory emotion.[10]

Primitive thought, it has been argued, is not, for Breton, the exclusive reserve of any particular racial group; "rather it is an intellectual category designating a way of thinking that is appropriate to all people but has been denigrated in the West, according to Michael Richardson."[11] Nonetheless, Breton and others of the era, rapt by *l'art nègre* and primitivism— the stuff of modernism—did share in the idea that people of color, "passive" in the creation of technological devices that led to modernization, capitalism, two world wars, and countless human casualties and suffering, were more in touch with the id. In this vein, then, surrealism shared in Negritude's essentializing tendencies around black existence and the primitive. Oppression, through arrests, exile, torture, and even murder of surrealist adherents during the war, also led to common experiences of marginality. It is especially perhaps that "feeling of uprooting and ensuing alienation," as Nardal writes, experienced by these black intellectuals during their time in Paris and André Breton's own forced exile to New York via Martinique in 1941 that contributed to a certain affinity.[12]

Yet, despite such affinities, *Tropiques* is as much a panblack or Negritude journal as it is a "journal of international surrealism."[13] The first issue had already appeared in Martinican bookstores when the Césaires encountered Breton in 1941. René Ménil writes in his introduction to the 1978 reissue of *Tropiques*, "Pour une lecture critique de *Tropiques*":

> Thus, the debt to surrealism, which is explicitly proclaimed in various places within the texts, must not paralyze analysis nor encourage lazy, mechanistic interpretations. . . . Breton notes, upon reading the first

issue of *Tropiques,* that the texts collected are clearly oriented . . . towards the same ends. . . . The texts in *Tropiques* reflect, in effect, not one and the same philosophy, but diverse philosophies in which some of them are closely related, and others are opposed and frankly contradictory. . . . What shocks us today is that these oppositions, these differences and these contradictions in philosophical conceptions remained unperceived by us. . . . *Tropiques* was the expression of the perspectives, of the hopes, and of the will of the revolutionary Antillean left in the forties.[14]

With the writers of *Tropiques* resorting to coded language and metaphors, folklore, ethnology, and poetry to inspire critical thinking on the part of *Tropiques* readers under the Vichy-inspired, despotic circumstances, philosophical dissonance was inevitable. *Tropiques* was indisputably eclectic in its theoretical orientation by virtue of its "cannibalizing" of various ethnological texts, Schoelcherism, and New Negro philosophies into that philosophy of black humanism called Negritude, which in turn would later cannabilize surrealism to produce a uniquely Martinican Negritude-surrealist cultural philosophy; but *Tropiques* was also, and more importantly, as Ménil writes, "revolutionary" even in its philosophical inconsistencies.

In the 1978 reissued edition of *Tropiques,* Aimé Césaire weighed in on the surrealist question with respect to his poetry and the orientation of *Tropiques* in an interview with Jacqueline Leiner: "When Breton read the first three issues of *Tropiques,* he believed I was a surrealist. This was not entirely true or entirely false. . . . I will say that the meeting with Breton was a confirmation of the truth of which I had happened upon through my own reflections."[15] Whereas Ménil was rather consistently surrealist from his first essay, "Naissance de notre art," to his various references to the "marvelous" and Breton's *Manifestes,* Aimé Césaire seesawed between surrealism and Negritude. And Suzanne Césaire's writings, while lauding surrealism for giving "us back some of our possibilities" after the Breton encounter, equally interspersed this advocacy with Leo Frobenius's ethnology, a linchpin in Negritude's Africanist pronouncements, and delivered an incisive critique of a West Indian who "cannot accept his Negritude" in her last decisive essay, in 1945, "Le Grand camouflage." The contents in the eleven issues of *Tropiques* reveal a mixed bag of ideological and philosophical writings, including surrealist poetry and essays by the likes of Breton and Lucie Thésée, writings by black Cubans Alejo Carpentier and Lydia Cabrera, New Negro poets like Jean Toomer, and a review of surrealist Wilfredo Lam's plastic art. Reprints of Schoelcher's abolitionist texts and excerpts from Frobenius's *Histoire de la civilisation africaine* also appeared.

TROPIQUES: REVUE CULTURELLE, THE REMEDY FOR THE MARTINICAN CULTURAL VOID

The cultural review *Tropiques* made its debut in Fort-de-France, Martinique, in April 1941. The quarterly could be purchased at twelve francs per issue or forty francs for a year's subscription, increasing to twenty francs per issue and seventy-five francs for a year's subscription by 1945. Yearly subscriptions were rare, as students mostly comprised the readership. The review was funded primarily out of the pockets of the Césaires and Ménil. Serving as editor, Aimé Césaire spelled out lyrically the review's reason for being in the first issue, in "Présentation":

> Sterile and silent land. It is of ours that I am speaking. And my hearing measures by the Caribbean Sea the frightening silence of Man. . . . [H]ere the monstrous atrophy of voice . . . exceptional muteness. No city. No art. No poetry. No civilization in its true sense, that is, that projection of man upon the world; that modeling of the world by man; that minting of the universe into man's effigy.
>
> No city. No art. No poetry. Not one germ. Not one shoot. But the hideous leprosy of forgery. In truth, a sterile and mute land.
>
> But it is no longer the time of scrounging off the world. It is a question of saving it. It is time to gird one's loins like a valiant man.
>
> [T]he shadow gains ground. . . . However, we are those who say *no* to the shadow.
>
> Strong-willed men create a new light in the world.[16]

Césaire's "Présentation" reflects the previous criticisms of Antillean creativity. Sterility, imitation, and muteness were all charges articulated before in various essays and by various authors. The uniqueness of Césaire's critique lies in its poetic rendering of the artistic dilemma. Martinicans had left no individualized, distinguishable mark on the world in art, poetry, sciences, or philosophies (5). Their only sown seeds were those tilled by the hoe and cutlass. And even in that life-creating moment, the Martinican artist was unable to capture that "feeling of the cane cutter." *Tropiques*'s contributors were those strong-willed men and women who would bring a new light into the world through poetry, art, and criticism; they would create a civilization in its truest sense where there was but a parasitic shell. *Tropiques* would save Martinique from its deliberately cultivated artistic mediocrity. In saying no to the shadow, the review's writers would refuse to mirror or ape French aesthetics, to reflect back in their blackness metropolitan aesthetics and norms. Césaire's "Présentation" announces the arrival of a new artistic contingent while declaring the end of the parroting material productions nurtured by French colonialism. The articulation of the "no" reflects a rejection as well as the proclamation of an individuality, a specificity outside of the colonial lockstep of France and its Antillean shadow. The verbalization of the "no" represents the liberation of the artist's voice hitherto reduced to a parodying echo.

The poetry, prose, and criticism in *Tropiques*'s first issue, perhaps its most thematically consistent issue, coalesce around Martinican self-discovery, recovery, and the creation of a new art. The metaphor of the shadow is ever-present. Aimé Césaire the poet does what he does best—expose the sterility of Martinican culture through a lyricism wed to Paulette Nardal's 1932 essay. Suzanne Césaire launches her literary career with an analysis called "Léo Frobenius et le problème des civilisations," which wrap ups with the claim that poetry is the philosophy advocated by Frobenius, a philosophy that allows for the recreation of the world with new experiences. In rejecting the shadow in order to present these new experiences, this regenerative, "fecund" philosophy that is poetry demands that the Martinican writer "dare to know oneself, dare to admit who one is, dare to ask what one wants to be." "It is time," she writes in her most mimetic moment, "to gird one's loins like a valiant man."[17]

René Ménil, the third voice of the newly formed *Tropiques* triumvirate, weighs in with his meditative essay "Naissance de notre art": "Every being is enclosed in its specificity. This is why human manifestations, acts, passions, dreams, are inseparably attached to man. Such are cultural expressions, the most durable and the most perfect of these manifestations. The culture of man, it is mankind in its social expressions."[18] Ménil sets up his argument regarding Martinican art in very general terms by first explaining that cultural expressions are representative of mankind in its specificity. The particularity and inimitability of a culture is expressed to the social world through its creative productions.

"Real culture," as opposed to the intellectual abstraction "the idea of culture," is "made up of a set of determined living conditions (land, race, economic forms, etc.), which is mitigated by all the contingencies of everyday life, that are concretely lived by the human individual" (55). Quite simply, for Ménil, culture is not detachable except as an abstraction or an idea. Attempts to separate individuals from the specificity of their cultural expressions require that each individual emerge from the self. The result is an illusion, an imitation; and "to imitate," Ménil suggests, "is to want to be the other" (55). In the realm of art, the more the individual puts himself or herself into the work, the more evocative the work. Menil concludes, then, that

> [a]rt tries to bring about the penetration and apprehension of the real: its point of departure is within impressions and images formed in our sensory perception of the world and which make up a singular life. . . . The artist does not have to overexert himself in order to express the world: he has only to come to terms with himself in order to express everything, being as he is, coextensive with the world in his poetic attitude. (56, 58)

Here again Ménil stresses the artist's role as an interpreter, as a seer into the world in which he or she coexists. Expressions of the artist's social world, bound up with culture, should be effortless from this standpoint, as that world is deeply anchored in the artist's being; it inhabits the artist, and the artist brings it forth through material productions.

After a lengthy contemplation on existence and expression, Ménil turns his attention to Martinicans,

> [a] people who have behind them three centuries of Recitation and who have always come to the courts of Culture empty-handed, having never produced anything. . . . All our cultural manifestations, within the domain of art, have been up to this day only pastiches. . . . Thus, this necessarily sterile imitation has brought us only worthless "works" . . . worthless, because they are not viable being products against nature. . . . Can we decently come to the rendezvous of art with, in our hands, the borrowed graces of a borrowed poetry? . . . It's time for the shadows to return to the shadows. (59–61)

Martinican people, having endured three centuries of slavery and the colonial system in which assimilation, acculturation, imitation, and recitation of things French had been their sole goal, had made no contributions to arts and letters. The bell of cultural void clangs once again in Ménil's blistering summation of the valuelessness of Martinican artistic expressions. In imitation, quality flees, he continues. Martinican poetry, literature, and art are but mere copies—and poorer copies at that—of those writers for whom French culture is not detachable, or alien. Only Léon Damas's *Pigments,* written in 1935, is offered as an example of poetry steeped in the particularity of the Antillean experience. Like Baudelaire, Ménil suggests that the birth of original art in Martinique requires candor, a reconciliation of the self with the repressed imagination, with the culture of the living, breathing dynamism that is uniquely Martinican.

Tropiques's conceptual depth, breadth, and subversive artistic politics did not escape Vichy officials on the island. The island's bourgeoisie also opposed the review and pressed for its discontinuation. In 1943, an explosive standoff occurred between the editors and Vichy officials. In a letter to Aimé Césaire dated May 10, 1943, Lieutenant Bayle, *chef du service d'information,* forbade the publication of the review by withholding printing paper. In returning the manuscripts scheduled for publication, he accused the contributors of trying "to poison minds, to sow hatred, to destroy morals." *Tropiques* was not a "literary or cultural review," he continued, but a "revolutionary, racial, and sectarian review."[19] Disconcerted by the review's republication of Schoelcher's texts, Bayle insisted that, since the abolitionists' era, "France has engaged in a politics of racial equality that it has not just proclaimed, but which it has also more sweepingly put into practice than any other country." Bayle deduced that Schoelcher "would be quite surprised to see his name and words used for the profit of such a cause" (xxxviii). Undeterred by Bayle's letter and refusal to grant the paper necessary to print *Tropiques,* Aimé and Suzanne Césaire, Georges Gratiant, Aristide Maugée, René Ménil, and Lucie Thésée responded in a laconic one-page letter two days later, on May 12, in which they cataloged all and sundry invectives used by Bayle to describe the review and its editorial collective: "racists," "sectarians," "revolutionaries," "ingrates and traitors to the fatherland," "poisoners of minds."[20] The collective drew comparisons between their agenda and that of other revolutionary thinkers. If they were *"ingrates and traitors,"* then they embodied the spirits of Zola, who denounced the "reactionary press"; *"revolutionaries,'* like Victor Hugo who wrote the 'Châtiments'"; and "'*[s]ectarians*,' passionately so, like Rimbaud and Lautréamont" (xxxvix). Their racism, they concluded, was the racism of Toussaint Louverture, Claude McKay, and Langston Hughes rather than that of Drumont and Hitler. Volumes 8 and 9 of *Tropiques* were combined in the sixth issue, published in October of that year. And in that issue, which further rattled Lieutenant Bayle, Suzanne Césaire defiantly challenged the authoritarian state of affairs on the island and declared that surrealism was in the service of liberty at the time, "when liberty itself is threatened throughout the world."[21]

THE EXPANSE OF SURREALISM AND NEGRITUDE

April 1942 marked the one-year anniversary of *Tropiques*. Over the course of its history, Suzanne Césaire had published four articles, on varied topics from Frobenius's ethnology to André Breton's poetry. For the review's one-year anniversary issue (although it did not proclaim the April 1942 issue as such), she contributed the first of three of the most pioneering and provocative essays of her short-lived literary career, "Malaise d'une civilisation." Cultural sterility expressed in the domain of Martinican art and literature as a theme predominates, and World War II functions as an analytical backdrop. In this essay Césaire situates the dilemma within the critical interstices of Frobenius's theories on culture, race, and ecology and Breton's automatic writing.

The German ethnologist made significant impressions on the young black students in Paris upon their first reading of his reprinted essay on spiritism in Central Africa in *La Revue du monde noir*.[22] As Léopold Senghor admits in "Lessons of Leo Frobenius," his preface to an anthology of Frobenius's collected works: "We knew by heart Chapter II of the first book of the *History*, entitled 'What Does Africa Mean to Us?' a chapter adorned with lapidary phrases such as this: 'The idea of the "barbarous Negro" is a European invention, which in turn dominated Europe until the beginning of this century.'"[23] Senghor continues: "Leo Frobenius was the one, above all others, who shed light for us on concepts such as *emotion, art, myth, Eurafrica*" (vii).

Frobenius combined the four branches of science—history, archaeology, ethnography, and cultural morphology—in his study of the meaning and phenomena of culture. For the Negritude writers, in regard to Frobenius's valuing of concepts such as emotion and intuition, "concepts," Senghor asserts, "or synonyms which we confront when we are considering Negroes . . . It is easy to guess the consequences of this discovery and the increased self-confidence which it gave us" (x–xi). Creating such terms as *paideuma,* the "spiritual essence of culture in general," or the "soul," Frobenius divided civilizations into two categories: Ethiopian and Hamitic. These civilizations subscribed to different methods of interpreting reality: "intuitive" or "mechanistic."[24] Such a division was neither racial nor quantified as superior or inferior, for Frobenius maintained that all cultures possess degrees of one category or the other and that the German soul approximated the Ethiopian essence or style. The ethnologist elaborates upon these ideas:

> The mechanistic approach is nowadays very much in vogue, and the intuitive correspondingly rare. . . . Both, in their way, are comprehensive, penetrating, almost compulsive modes of thought, with their own claim to interpret reality. Nor am I suggesting that there is anything especially new or superior about the intuitive method. As for novelty, Goethe himself took a thoroughly intuitive view of the world, . . . so that he was not wrong in predicting that his work would never be popular—even though tags from *Faust* are on everybody's lips. As for superiority, every culture we know has oscillated between the two poles of mechanism and intuition. . . . However, in advancing the theory that we are moving into a new cultural era, the advent of which can be felt rather than proved, I am bound to support the revival of an intuitive attitude.
>
> It must also be stressed that there is no such thing as an absolutely mechanistic or an absolutely intuitive outlook. It is a question rather of the predominance of one or other of two tendencies.[25]

Hence, the Ethiopian style apprehends reality intuitively rather than mechanistically, is prone to emotion, and is given over to the creation of myths, art, and poetry. The Ethiopian style is one of abandon, of harmony with nature, whereas the Hamitic style, preoccupied with the domination of nature, is one of struggle. Moreover, according to Frobenius, civilizations do not progress in a linear fashion from primitivity to modernity, nor does humankind create or perfect civilization. Civilization develops in manifold directions, in a nonlinear fashion, through the shock or surge of the paideuma in its interaction with living species. Each shock, writes Frobenius in his *Histoire de la civilisation africaine,* occasions "new sentiments of life," and "the history of civilization is the history of transformations of the sentiments of life."

In following Frobenius's morphology of cultures, Suzanne Césaire's premise in "Malaise d'une civilisation" is that the war is a "paideumaic" surge or shock, an "inexorable pressure of destiny that will dip the whole world in blood in order, tomorrow, to give it its new face."[26] As imperialist and catastrophic as these "troubling times" are, they are, importantly, the horrific catalyst of a new humanism, a new art in Martinique, where the "suffering, sensitive, sometimes mocking being" pervasive in Martinique's folkloric traditions will be represented "in Martinique's ordinary literary products" (43). The present war-torn age, Césaire seemingly contends, cannot but reshape Martinican destiny in terms of the self and culture. But before this new date with destiny can be realized, Martinique, so long in the shadow of Frenchness that a malaise has gripped its soul, must be cured via an unearthing of its true self. Frobenius again proves useful as Césaire begins "Malaise d'une civilisation" by exploring the topographical nature and geographical position of the island and their relationships to the Martinican personality and the paucity of authentic art and literature.

Martinique is "the Tropics," she notes. Despite reprehensible living conditions and obscene mortality rates, imported Africans adapted because of the similiarity rather than dissimiliarity of the island's climate to their homeland. And yet this adeptness at climatic adapting, at survival over centuries of economic, social, and political depravation by Martinican people, has not resulted in a production of "authentic works of art." "How," Césaire asks, "is it that over the centuries no viable survivors of the original styles have been revealed—for example, those styles that have flowered so magnificently on African soil? Sculptures, ornate fabrics, paintings, poetry?" (44). Refuting the imbecilic claims that attribute "climate," "inferiority," or "instinct for laziness, theft, wickedness" to Martinican artistic torpor, Césaire insightfully argues:

> [I]t is explained, I believe, as follows, by:
>
> (1) the horrific conditions of being brutally transplanted onto a foreign soil; we have too quickly forgotten the slave ships and the sufferings of our slave fathers. Here, forgetting equals cowardice.
>
> (2) an obligatory submission, under pain of flogging and death, to a system of "civilization," a "style" even more foreign to the new arrivals than the tropical land.
>
> (3) finally, after the liberation of people of color, through a collective

error about our true nature, an error born of the following idea, anchored in the deepest recesses of popular consciousness by centuries of suffering: "Since the superiority of the colonizers arises from a certain style of life, we can access power only by mastering the techniques of this 'style' in our turn."

Let's stop and measure the importance of this gigantic mistake. (44–45)

Martinican cultural inertia is multiply rooted. The horrors of the Middle Passage are evoked; the life-threatening and "style"-altering processes of cultural immersion that required a repression of one's name, country, family, clan, language, and culture, and the atrocities of chattel slavery are cited as explanations; but perhaps the most damaging factor, in Césaire's view, has been the mastery of the French "style" as a result of centuries of compelled submission. For Suzanne Césaire, there are apparent inconsistencies in Martinicans' authentic style or self and the life they lead in 1942 as a result of slavery and colonialism. The conflict in the Martinican psyche must be ferreted out for a better understanding of just who Martinicans really are and who they have become as a result of various historical processes. Again turning to Frobenius, Césaire asks, "What is the Martinican?" "A human plant" is the response (45). Martinicans coexist peacefully rather than antagonistically with nature; Martinicans abandon themselves to the "rhythm of universal life." In this comparison, Césaire debunks at once the stereotype of the "lazy" Martinican. The Martinican "vegetates"; his or her favorite phrase is "let it flow" (45). In heading off any assumptions regarding Martinican passivity, Césaire follows up by relating that independence and tenacity are also characteristics of the plant, and thus of Martinicans. Despite being trampled upon, yanked, and pulled out of the land by its roots, the Martinican-cum-plant persists. The plant as a leitmotiv for the Martinican way of life further reflects, according to Césaire, island folklore: after the birth of a child, the placenta is interred among the coconut or banana trees; grass growing on a grave is a sign of the dead protesting death (45). Martinicans have forgotten their nature, their true self; hence, for Césaire, the cultural malaise, sterility, and discontent of the civilization. She continues: "[T]he Martinican has failed because, misrecognizing his true nature, he tries to live a life that is not suited to him. A gigantic phenomenon of collective lying, of 'pseudomorphosis.' And the current state of civilization in the Caribbean reveals to us the consequences of this error. Repression, suffering, sterility" (46).

The loss of the self naturally occurred as a result of the adaptation to oppressive sociohistorical and economic conditions. In providing a brief overview of Martinican history, Césaire reminds her reader that Martinicans, both métis and black, were socially, politically, and culturally disenfranchised. Assimilation was initially strictly forbidden, but deference to whites was demanded as early as 1764. By 1788 the primary occupation open to free men of color was manual labor, "the hoe and the cutlass." The abolition of slavery did not result in the opening up of economic avenues for Martinicans on the island. Under the colonial system, the island was still deeply wedded to a plantation-like, agrarian economy; its primary function continued to be as an exporter of primary products. Martinicans, although resistant to the circumscription of their labor and talents, were again tied to the field as low-paid wage laborers. As author Joseph Zobel wrote in his coming-of-age novel *La Rue Cases-Nègres,* the *patron,* or the boss, had merely replaced the master.[27] Work permits were required for those wishing to indulge in other occupational areas. The attendant effect of systematic second-class citizenship was the desire for first-class citizenship with the macabre twist that the latter became narrowly defined through a prism of Frenchness. An almost slavish desire for assimilation to Frenchness preoccupied the psychic impulses of Martinicans. "Liberation" disastrously became equated with "assimilation."

The psychic drive for assimilation, most evident among the "colored bourgeoisie," according to Césaire, definitively suppressed the Ethiopian sentiment of life, the desire for abandon, and replaced it with the Hamitic desire for struggle. In Freudian terms, the true Martinican self, the Ethiopian sentiment, is buried deep within the unconscious, the id, whereas the Hamitic desire for struggle occupies the conscious and preconscious, the ego and the superego. As Césaire remarks: "The race to riches. To diplomas. Ambition. Struggle reduced to the level of the bourgeoisie. The race to monkey-like imitations. Vanity fair"—all are representative of Hamitic culture.[28] But more troubling is that the imitative desire clearly perceived among those conscious Martinicans is wholly repressed in the unconscious of those in hot pursuit of Frenchness. Like a clinician observing and diagnosing her patient, in this case Martinican civilization, Césaire concludes:

No "evolved" Martinican would accept that he is only imitating, so much does his current situation appear natural, spontaneous, born of his most legitimate aspirations. And, in so doing, he would be sincere. He truly does not KNOW that he is imitating. He is *unaware* of his true nature, which does not cease to exist. . . .

Just as the *hysteric* is unaware that he is merely *imitating* an illness but the doctor, who cares for him and delivers him from his morbid symptoms, knows it.

Likewise, analysis shows us that the effort to adapt to a foreign style that is demanded of the Martinican does not take place without creating a state of pseudocivilization that can be qualified as *abnormal, teratoid.* (47–48; Césaire's italics)

Suzanne Césaire uses the French concept of *évolué* to describe imitating, assimilated Martinicans. They believe sincerely that they have "evolved" to Frenchness, that they are French, when instead they are imitating Frenchness. The energy Martinicans have expended in this struggle against the self has been rewarded with the creation of an imitative civilization; a France in the Caribbean that is not really French but a copy; a mere *shadow* of the original.

The lengthy analysis of Martinican civilization's psychosis naturally concludes where it began—in a turn toward the cultural. In searching for the cure to cultural sterility, Césaire endeavors to determine whether the "essence" of Martinicans buried in the unconscious, the primacy of the plant and the Ethiopian sentiment, can be rechanneled to create "a viable, hence imposing, cultural style." Césaire calls upon her readers—future artists, poets, and intellectuals—to recognize their true, inner selves, to become inspired by these tropical lands and produce an authentic culture and authentic arts. Surrealism is here evoked as a means through which to tap that inner self. Surrealism, with its emphasis on writing from the unconscious, "gave us back some of our possibilities," Césaire writes. "It is up to us to find the rest. By its guiding light" (48). Surrealism will become a tool for the exploration of what is authentically Martinican, and Negritude will initiate the coming into race conscious among these potential bards of Martiniquan culture. Despite recognizing the connection to Africa—that Ethiopian sentiment essential to tapping into the self—here Suzanne Césaire makes a critical theoretical move toward the cultural and racial *métissage,* hitherto repressed by the privileging of the Hamitic culture, that best characterizes Martinican civilization:

> Understand me well:
> It is not a question of a return to the past, of resurrecting an African past that we have learned to appreciate and respect. On the contrary, it is a question of mobilizing every living force mingled together on this land where race is the result of the most continuous brazing; it is a question of becoming conscious of the tremendous heap of various energies we have until now locked up within ourselves. We must now put them to use in their fullness, without deviation and without falsification. (48)

Césaire's emphasis is on present realities, not the past. And yet the conscious recognition of that past is essential to reaching the inner self and recreating a new postwar world.

LIBERATORY POETICS, MÉTISSAGE, AND DIVERSITY

In her essay in the 1945 issue of *Tropiques,* which marked the end of the cultural review's publication run as well as Suzanne Césaire's contributions to Martinican letters and apparently to public life, the enigmatic Césaire interestingly has the last word. Her essay closes out the combined volume 13–14 of *Tropiques.* Whether domestic responsibilities overtook her activism, or her husband's increasing presence and celebrity in French and Martinican political and literary life during the postwar period became the familial priority, Suzanne Césaire's essay "Le Grand camouflage" represents her final effort to expand the theoretical parameters of Negritude's Africanist identity politics. This last essay professed that the originality, diversity, and plurality of Martinican culture and its people were well embodied in the "femmes-colibris, femmes-fleurs tropicales, femmes aux quatre races et aux douzaines de sang" [hummingbird-women, tropical flower–women, the women of four races and dozens of bloodlines].[29] It also presented the dismal social and political realities in the Antilles in general and Martinique in particular.

"Le Grand camouflage" could very well be entitled "The Great Smoke Screen," as Césaire takes the reader on a rather sublime but violent tour of Caribbean topography; the productive life forces of exploding volcanoes, turbulent cyclones, and earthquakes; and "the beautiful green waves" [belles lames vertes] of the Caribbean Sea (267). From Puerto Rico to Martinique to Haiti, a billowing and swirling cyclone pummels the islands. But this is, we are to understand, nature's way; the ebb and flow of life on the islands. When the storm passes, the beauty of the islands reappears. This incomparable splendor, "perfect colors and forms" (269), is what the Caribbean has come to represent. With eyes of an enraptured tourist or a blind Antillean native, Césaire writes:

> Nevertheless, fifteen years ago, the Antilles were revealed to me from the flank of Mount Pelée. From here I discovered, though still very young, that Martinique was sensual, coiled up, extended, distended into the Caribbean Sea, and I thought about the other islands that are so beautiful.
>
> Once again in Haiti, during the summer mornings of 1944, I experienced the presence of the Antilles, more perceptible in places from which, like at Kenscoff, the mountain views are of an unbearable beauty. (268–69)

And yet there is and has always been trouble in these paradisaical isles, pain and pangs accompanying their beauty. A legacy of slavery, colonialism, and modern capitalism has effectively altered the balance between humanity and the island's natural beauty, harnessing first the slave and then the worker to the land; fusing racism, wage labor, and class exploitation into modern capitalism. The naive vision of a Martinican girl and the cataractous eyes of a woman in Haiti in 1944 have been replaced with the wide-eyed sagacity of a Pan-Africanist theorist: "And now, total lucidity. Beyond these perfect colors and forms, my gaze detects the innermost torments in the Antilles' most beautiful face" (269). The complex history of the Americas, the New World (if such a term is appropriate in light of the New World's newness only to Europe and not to its indigenous populations of Caribs and Arawak), is laid out for the reader's contemplation. From the conquistadors' importing the technology of firearms to "the slave trade's infamy" and colonialism, the Americas and their annihilated aboriginal and forcibly imported populations have been reduced to the economic, social, psychological, and political whims of a European-descended population of "adventurous demons," "convicts," "penitents," and "utopians" "belched forth" to various corners of the New World (269).

Césaire's diasporic accounting of black exploitation and affliction moves through the Caribbean to the United States and then back to the Francophone West Indian situation in 1945. The ideals of the abolitionist Victor Schoelcher regarding the status of blacks in the postplantation economies of the colonies are contrasted with the reality of the "refined forms of slavery" masked in its "degrading forms of modern wage labor." The Francophone Caribbean is, according to Césaire, "a stain" on France's face (269). Her historical analysis of the coming-into-being of an exploited black world paves the way for a sociological analysis of the island of Martinique. Césaire provides the reader with great insight into the interlocking and complex race, color, and class structure dominating Martinique. Martinique comprises *békés,* or white Creoles, white French "metropolitan officials," "the colored bourgeoisie," and the black working class ("les travailleurs") (270–72).

"[T]he human deprivation of the Antilles" is attributed to the *békés.* Born on the island, they feel not wholly French, because of their "drawling accent" and "unsure French"—almost assuredly a result of their intermingling with their patois-speaking "black *da[s]*"—and certainly not Martinican, because of its "colored" connotations (270). The *békés* belong primarily to the merchant and managerial classes, those "false colonizers" whose exploitation of the black working class results in drastically low wages in the plantation economy of factories and drastically high prices for goods purchased in the marketplace. The moral bankruptcy and cowardliness of this class is, for Césaire, handily demonstrated through their collaborationist past:

> Ready to betray any and all in order to defend themselves against the rising tide of blacks, they would sell themselves to America were it not that the Americans claim that the purity of their blood is highly suspect, just as in the 1940s they devoted themselves to the Admiral of Vichy: Pétain being for them the altar of France, Robert necessarily became "the tabernacle of the Antilles." (270)

Césaire delivers a two-pronged critique—one of the United States and the other of the *békés.* The race-purity-obsessed narratives of America confirm the very fears of the white Creoles—the perception that they are not white by virtue of their proximity to blacks. The U.S. narrative is necessarily fraught with contradictions, given the associations of blacks and whites during chattel slavery in the North and South and despite the legalized segregation of the *Plessy v. Ferguson* era. The end of slavery in the United States gave way to a rise in black women domestic workers— the equivalent of the *da* in the Antilles—in white American households.

The *béké* class also suffers from French exoticism, whereby they are rendered strange because of their place of birth, yet familiar because of their "white" skin. The white Creole bears the brunt of American perceptions of France's racial liberalism—a liberalism that importantly encompassed, in the American mind, sexual intimacy, and thus "colored" ancestry. Césaire implies that the *békés* are persons with no veritable country, no feeling of belonging, no concept of patriotism or of *la République française,* which would explain why they could unabashedly pledge themselves to the wrong France—the *état français* of Vichy.

The island's other white racial and class grouping consists of metropolitan French functionaries. For them, Césaire cynically suggests, color prejudice is nonexistent. And yet there is a fear and loathing upon contact with "our 'old French lands'":

> When they look into the maleficent mirror of the Caribbean, they see a delirious image of themselves. They dare not recognize themselves. . . . They know that the métis share some of their blood, that they are also, like them, part of Western civilization. . . . But their colored descendants fill them with dread. . . . They did not expect that strange burgeoning of their blood. Perhaps they didn't want to answer the Antillean heir who does and does not cry out "my father." (270–71)

The Antillean human landscape of racial *métissage* and cultural assimilation is overwhelming for the metropolitans. The Martinicans are, importantly, the "unexpected sons" and "charming daughters" of France. Césaire begs the question regarding the nature of the unexpectedness in light of centuries of intermingling (sexual and social, coercive and consensual) and cultural importation (also coercive, at least initially). The Martinicans are French, yet they do not hold the "title of citizen" (269–71). Their muffled voice but volumes-speaking métis existence demands recognition in the most literal sense of paternity, from *la patrie* and *le père.* France has inseminated the island. Césaire's patriarchal emphasis, the masculinized embodiment of France, is undeniably deliberate; neither *mère* [mother] nor *mère-patrie* [motherland] is evoked. The Hegelian master-slave dialectic is color-coded and sexualized, with France representing the white male master and Martinique the subjugated black female slave. Indeed, Frantz Fanon would write in 1967 that "[i]n the colonies, in fact, even though there is little marriage or actual sustained cohabitation between whites and blacks, the number of hybrids is amazing. This is because the white men often sleep with their black servants."[30]

Suzanne Césaire certainly elaborated this theme in her discussion of the *naissance* of the colored bourgeoisie. "Here is an Antillean," she writes, "the great-grandson of a colonist and a black slave woman."[31] He has inherited the "courage" of "African warriors," in their eternal life-and-death struggles, and the "greed" of the colonists. This West Indian tussles with his identity. He is not white, although he desires complete immersion in whiteness, and he will not "accept his Negritude": "Here he is with his double force and double ferociousness, in a dangerous equilibrium." He is a member of the "colored bourgeoisie"; running the island with a smooth efficiency, he placates and attends to white interests by exploiting the needs of the black workers—a true comprador. "So blossoms in the Antilles," she concludes, "that flower of human baseness, the colored bourgeoisie" (271).

And the black working class, indubitably made up of slaves to the machine, is varyingly seduced by the "automobile de grand luxe" and the "usines-claires" [brightly lit factories]. Returning to the Frobenius-inspired vegetal imagery regarding Martinicans and articulating a Marxist zeal, Suzanne Césaire visualizes "an invisible vegetation of desire" within the black workers, from whom a "Revolution will inevitably spring forth" (271). As a plant people, a vegetal people, who at once flow seamlessly with life and resist systematic destruction, the workers are one with the land; the land exists, suffers, and resists just as the masses of people do. That poet who merely passes by will nonetheless continue to be ensnared by the beauty of the tropical landscape, "that sweet sound of palms," while "the Antillean serf lives with misery and abjection on the grounds of the 'factory,' and the mediocre state of our cities-towns is a nauseating spectacle" (270).

By the concluding paragraphs of "Le Grand camouflage," Césaire imagines that the Antillean poet will take up his place as an *engagé* and catch a glimpse of that "vegetal fire," his head reeling. He will contrast that wondrous *paysage* of cicadas, frangipani, cannas, gerberas, hibiscuses, and bougainvilleas and those who work the land, and will see "the hungers, fears, hatreds, and ferocity that burn in the hollows of hills." Only the poet, whose eyes alone are "able to see," will unmask the game of *cache-cache*, hide-and-seek, the "great camouflage" (273). The poet's "tongue," as Aimé Césaire writes in *Cahier d'un retour au pays natal*, will "serve those miseries which have no tongue"; his "voice [will be] the liberty of those who founder in the dungeons of despair,"[32] the interpreter and interlocutor of the collective conscience, a liberatory resource who will present the island's history, pain, and exploitation. And that day when the smoke has cleared, the fog has lifted, and the silent vapors of the Caribbean Sea have evaporated via the will of the masses and the poet's pen and voice will certainly, Suzanne Césaire concludes, "be too enchanting for us to see."[33]

Edited and Annotated Translations
T. Denean Sharpley-Whiting and Georges Van Den Abbeele

Black Internationalism

Jane Nardal

There is in this postwar era a lowering or the attempt at a lowering of the barriers that exist between countries. Will the various frontiers, custom duties, prejudices, cultural mores, religion, and languages allow this project to be realized? We want to hope for this, those of us who note at the same time the birth of a movement not at all opposed to this first one. Blacks of all origins, of different nationalities, mores, and religions vaguely feel that in spite of everything they belong to one and the same race. Previously the more assimilated blacks looked down arrogantly upon their colored brethren, believing themselves surely of a different species than they; on the other hand, certain blacks who had never left African soil to be led into slavery looked down upon as so many base swine those who at the whim of whites had been enslaved, then freed, then molded into the white man's image.

Then came war, dislocation, blacks from every origin coming together in Europe, the sufferings of the war, the similar infelicities of the postwar period. Then snobs—whom we must thank here—and artists launched Negro art. They taught many blacks, who themselves were surprised, that there existed in Africa an absolutely original black literature and sculpture, that in America poetry and sublime songs, "the Spirituals," had been composed by wretched black slaves. Successively revealed to the white world as well as the black was the plasticity of black bodies in their sculptural attitudes, giving way without transition to an undulation, or to a sudden slackening, under the rule of rhythm, the sovereign master of their bodies; in this black face, so mysterious to whites, the artist would discover tones so shifting and expressions so fleeting as to make either his joy or his despair; the cinema, the theater, the music hall opened their doors to the conquering blacks.

All these reasons—from the most important to the most futile—must be taken into account to explain the birth among Negroes of a race spirit. Henceforth there would be some interest, some originality, some pride in being Negro, in turning back toward Africa, the cradle of Negroes, in remembering a common origin. The Negro would perhaps have his part to play in the concert of the races, where until now, weak and intimidated, he has kept quiet.

From these new ideas, new words, whence the creative significance of the terms: Afro-American, Afro-Latin. They confirm our thesis while casting new meaning on the nature of this Black Internationalism. If the Negro wants to know himself, assert his personality, and not be the copy of this or that type from another race (which often earns him contempt and mockery), it does not follow from that, however, that he becomes resolutely hostile to all contributions made by another race. On the contrary, he must learn to profit from others' acquired experience and intellectual wealth, but in order to know himself better and to assert his personality. To be Afro-American, to be Afro-Latin, means to be an encouragement, a consolation, an example for the blacks of Africa by showing them that certain benefits of white civilization do not necessarily lead to a rejection of one's race.

Africans, on the other hand, could profit from this example by reconciling these teachings with the millennial traditions of which they are justly proud. For it no longer comes into the head of the cultivated man to treat them en masse as savages. The work of sociologists has made known to the white world the centers of African civilization, their religious systems, their forms of government, their artistic wealth. Hence the bitterness they feel for having been despoiled is understandable and can be attenuated by that peculiar effect of the colonization: that of linking together, of unifying in a racial solidarity, and, in spite of the feuds between the conquering peoples, tribes who hadn't the slightest idea in this regard.

Along this barely trodden path, American blacks have been the pioneers, I believe. To convince oneself of this, it suffices to read *The New Negro* by Alain Locke, which is slated to appear in French translation by Payot.

The obstacles they encountered (late emancipation, economic slavery still existing in the South, humiliations, lynchings) were so many incentives. And in business and industry, as well as in the fine arts and literature, their successes are impressive, and above all—what interests us here—the prejudices of the whites who surround them have produced in them an unparalleled solidarity and race consciousness.

The Afro-Latins, in contact with a race less hostile to the man of color than the Anglo-Saxon race, have been for that reason retarded in this path. Their hesitation, what's more, is a credit to the country that understood that it should try its best to assimilate them. Even though their loyalty is reassuring, their love of the Latin country, the adoptive land, and their love of Africa, land of their ancestors, are not incompatible. The Negro spirit, so supple, so capable of assimilation, so discerning, will easily surmount this apparent difficulty. And already, helped, encouraged by black American intellectuals, the young Afro-Latins, distinguishing themselves from the preceding generation, hastening to catch the masses up with those who are evolving in that effect, will go beyond them in order the better to guide them. In tending to this task, formed in European methods, they will take advantage of these methods in order to study the spirit of their race, the past of their race with all the necessary critical verve. That black youth are already taking on the study of slavery, facing up to, with detachment, a past that is quite palpable and so painful—isn't that the greatest proof that there does finally exist a black race, a race spirit on the path of maturity? Those who know how, among black people, certain subjects have until recently been taboo can appraise the progress represented by these recent facts.

Originally published as "Internationalisme noir," *La Dépêche africaine,* February 15, 1928, 5.

Exotic Puppets

Jane Nardal

Regarding the evocative power of certain words, the Creole who has spent time in France can readily testify. Should it come to be known or perceived that you are "exotic," you will arouse a lively interest, preposterous questions, the dreams and regrets of those who have never traveled: "Oh! The golden Islands! the marvelous lands! with their happy, naive, carefree natives!" In vain, you strive to destroy so many legends they hardly believe you: so much so that you reproach yourself for trying to destroy illusions profoundly anchored in the French mind and fallen from literature into the public domain.

As with Léon Werth, when he writes in *Danses, danseurs, et dancings*: "So it is that I perceived black woman. I am not sure that she wasn't already outfitted with a bookish poetry. Perhaps it is that she was first a literary Negress, a princess and sultana. The island novels and *A Thousand and One Nights*. But it is not my fault, if that flexible grace became a part of literature or rather if she became a kind of sexual poetry, innate in us."

Shall we have the courage to divest ourselves of the prestige the literature of exoticism confers upon us and, as modernists, to clash with the past, rococo decor of hammocks, palm trees, virgin forests, etc.

What a deception for him who evokes exotic princesses in your honor, if you were to tell him, just like a little French girl of the middle classes, that you are in Paris pursuing studies that you began over there, in the Tropics, in high school? No, the rights of the imagination cannot be prescribed, you resign yourself to usurping that role, to being someone who comes from those faraway lands where everything is vibrantly afire: air, hearts, bodies.

Nevertheless, it seems that the box full of exotic accessories has been overturned, or at least that someone else has succeeded that pontiff, Bernardin de Saint-Pierre. It would be bad grace for us to complain about all the fuss made over Bernardin with his exotic and enchanting sites, full of idyllic creatures, the good savage, and the white man become innocent anew. Similarly, the great Romantic writers, Hugo, Lamartine, and Michelet, on the one hand; Mrs. Beecher Stowe, on the other, lay stress on the same point: for the needs of the humanitarian cause, the exotic character, in the occurrence the black slave, is adorned with every virtue—these writers engendered an abundant posterity.

Works like *L'Ulysse nègre* by Marius-Ary Leblond, a writer from Reunion Island; *The Nigger of the Narcissus* by Conrad; *Le Pot au noir* by Chadourne; [and] the tales of C. Farrère already seem to break with this tradition and claim to give a more truthful portrait of the colored man to sedentary and sentimental metropolitans.

But Josephine came, Josephine Baker you understand, and bored a hole through the painted backdrop associated with Bernardin. Here it is that a woman of color leaps onstage with her shellacked hair and sparkling smile. She is certainly still dressed in feathers and banana leaves, but she brings to Parisians the latest Broadway products (the Charleston, jazz, etc.). The transition between past and present, the soldering between virgin forest and modernism, is what American blacks have accomplished and rendered tangible.

And the blasé artists and snobs find in them what they seek: the savorous, spicy contrast of primitive beings in an ultramodern frame of African frenzy unfurled in the cubist decor of a nightclub. This explains the unprecedented vogue and the swell of enthusiasm generated by a little *capresse* who was begging on the sidewalks of St. Louis (Mississippi).[1]

For she and her friends (Joe Alex, Douglas Johnny, Hudgins), in the course of entertaining the Parisian public, offer new and truculent images for the avant-garde writers. In hearing their sweet and raucous melodies in concert, in the music hall, on records, these writers reconstitute a strange atmosphere where one still hears something reminiscent of the wailing of poor slaves with an aftertaste of naïveté and now and then savagery. Thus, in modern, exotic literature, the poetic imagination loses none of its prerogatives, even when it no longer awards the prize for excellence to good "Uncle Toms."

So, after the grenadine syrup of Bernardin and Beecher Stowe, here are the hard liquor and cocktails of Soupault, of Carl Van Vechten: Cover your face, Uncle Tom, up there; here is your grandson Edgar Manning, the hero of Soupault's novel, free and let loose in a civilization whose vices alone has he imitated; a jazz-band Negro, he leads an existence as nocturnal as it is sleazy, takes drugs, kills a woman. That's Soupault's Negro. These same character types and vices are found in Carl Van Vechten's *Nigger Heaven,* but in the New York world of billionaire blacks. The femme fatale represented there has nothing to do with the Romantic portrait of the black woman in Michelet. These writers have led the way; no doubt the Morands and company will fall into step. . . .

But, you tell me, what does this existence, which, it is true, is colorful, bustling, and intoxicating, have in common with our own, with its tranquil grace and slow dances, except the decor? Let the black Creoles not be surprised, since a new pontiff there is, to be so devoured by reporters and writers in a rush to generalize. Wait a little longer, and maybe they will be genuflecting before Claude Farrère.

Shall we pronounce ourselves for one or the other of these two pontiffs? With which sauce do we want to be eaten: the idealist sauce or the realist one? Here is the right answer—the American novelists of color, dismissing their portrayers, have put themselves to the task. We will one day see whether they have fared better.

We shall no longer go to the woods; the laurel trees have been cut down, the beautiful lady there has picked them all up. And, just like in the song, Paul Morand, having destroyed all the false ideas and illusions of the French when it comes to the subject of blacks, presents them with the revised and corrected stereotype of the "New Negro," as it has been represented to them from 1930 to 19 *[sic]* . . .

In a series of novellas, he presents in the following order (for he traveled over 50,000 kilometers and to 28 Negro countries): the Antillean black under the characteristics of the Haitian Occide, the black Czar who succeeds in delivering his country from the American yoke only to turn it into a soviet republic and bring back the Americans; the American Negro, represented by the dancing girl, Congo; a jazz musician; black leaders Octavius Bloom and Doctor Lincoln Vamp; and the mulatto multimillionaire Ms. Pamela Freedman; and finally, the African Negro into sorcery, fetishism, and cannibalism.

You will note that he is careful not to confuse these different stereotypes; he uses them only to show, invariably, at the end of each of his novellas, the power of Negro atavism. Whatever he be, black or almost white, well-schooled or illiterate, French, American, or in a state of savagery, in short, civilized in appearance, the Negro, if the occasion permits, will return to his instincts of superstition and magic.

I'm proposing this stereotype for your reflections. I leave to others the task of getting indignant about these various caricatures of blacks. I will simply note that this latter stereotype of Negroes, for those who have lived in France the last few years, was already latent in certain minds, in a certain milieu. Paul Morand did not invent it out of the blue—a few sharp observations bear this out. If the sociological works of Lévy-Bruhl, as he himself indicates, were his sources for the American Negro; if as I believe, he made extensive use of the *The New Negro* by Alain Locke (a man of color) to represent the American black, who gave him the stereotype for the black Antillean? Undoubtedly the Blomet Ball, analogous to our casinos, or worse—his stopovers of a few hours in the Antilles—perhaps some "quimboiseurs"—and literary stereotypes, like that of the dangerous mulatto. But above all—and I'm finally lighting my lantern—all the trouble comes from the fact that the vogue for Negroes these last few years has led to their being considered as folk destined to serve as amusement, to see to the pleasure, artistic or sensual, of whites (and in this regard Paul Morand gives just praise of Negro plasticity); but when it is a question of intellectual, or moral, qualities, when it is a question of no longer being their clown but their equal, that disturbs nature's plan and the viewpoints of providence. Thus, for aesthetic pleasure, Paul Morand and his consorts rely on or return to the state of nature, like Ms. Pamela Freedman. She has had enough of being a phony white woman? Why take pride in a borrowed progress? Having thought about this, she returns to the state of savagery.

Such is, then, the psychology of the Negro as depicted by the white, but what interests Paul Morand he himself tells us in an issue of *Candide*—July 12, 1928 ("The Age of the Negro," by P. Morand). "The Negro is our shadow," he writes again in his novel (page 206). This time I hope you will let out a sigh of relief. We have here not the portrait of the Negro, but that of the postwar European assimilated to the Negro, for which he feels shame: "Our era is a Negro era. Just think of the general slackness, the distaste of young people for hard work, the nudity, equality, fraternity, clay houses that last three years, public lovemaking, divorces, publicity, etc." (page 206).

Having made this clarification, may we not allow ourselves to praise the expository qualities and the clarity of P. Morand's style, a style that contains, moreover, such modern, original and fresh images, the backbones of the palm trees docile before the breeze smeared with moonlight—"Eighteen-carat stars" (p. 20). We even smile upon reading certain sentences where we see, indeed: "French, born sly." He notes the frequency of imperfect subjunctives, the absence of *a*'s from our speech—the coffee-and-cream anarchists of Chicago—or, again, "a face the color of stout foam," etc., and other gracious expressions: "Beforehand, Pamela was in the habit of saying like the others: 'Those awful blacks.'" He also notes how certain men of color can pass for being South American.

In short, after these amenities, we need to look really close to see, as if with regrets—it's no longer in fashion to be humanitarian, is it?—[that] a vague sympathy for blacks peeks through in sentences like the following: "the exploited, enslaved, beaten, martyred race who did not deserve its fate and who can hope for happiness only in the afterlife" (page 102). Or, again, despite its impassive tone, the following parenthetical utterance: "(Paris, the friend of Negroes, is not the Paris in Texas)," or this one: "[T]he aunt . . . recalled the South (United States) and its lynching trees" (page 158). Or the first chapters of the novella "Goodbye New York" (pages 209 and 211), where he strips bare the hypocrisy of Americans struggling with their racial prejudices. These pages must be kept in mind, stamped as they are with a very Latin frankness and humanity, if we are not to conclude, too quickly perhaps upon reading the novellas "Excelsior" and "Charleston," that everything gets Americanized. Paul Morand takes a real pleasure in being the door-to-door salesman in France of American prejudices.

"Before 1914," writes Paul Morand, "a black person was something laughable and exotic." Now, from the point of view of plasticity, he has made us come out ahead. The European admires him in the same way as a beautiful animal, with which he shares, like Congo the dancer (alias Josephine Baker), its suppleness, joy, and "immediately transmitted vital energy" (page 81). The conquest of the artist thus complete, it now remains for the European to do the same to the middle class, to the intellectuals. For that, we await some European to attribute certain, more inner qualities to the "literary" Negro, unless somewhere there already exists a painting of the Negro "seen from within," which would allow him to enter into the human community.

Originally published as "Pantins exotiques," *La Dépêche africaine,* October 15, 1928, 2.

Acts of Grace

Paulette Nardal

Do you realize what the return of spring, or rather summer, might be for an Antillean woman, having long lived in France?

It's first of all a feeling of relief. The heavy gray clouds, the persistent cold, the grim atmosphere of winter; it seemed to me that all that weighed on my chest, oppressed me. It was like an intolerable pain that I also by dint of habit came no longer to suffer.

It now seems that everything has become light, light. The warm air, the blue sky, the odors wafting from the trees and, especially, the sun finally triumphing over the grayness of winter; everything seems to me animated by a holy mirth.

I have a desire to walk, to run, in the gilded light. I want to be out in the country, to intoxicate myself with the odor of the earth, of the grass, to see the wet grass glistening in the sunlight and turning iridescent under the caresses of the breeze.

In my homeland, it's perpetual summer. The coconut trees with their heavy fruit lean toward the sea with its odors of seaweed, and the long tails of their leaflets rub against each other, like silk rustling. Standing before the delicate and uniform green of the chestnut trees in France, my thoughts evoke the somber mass of mango trees, breadfruit trees, sandbox and fern trees.

Is there not something passionate in the Antillean landscape, even in its most intimate and familiar sites far from the mountain, which the French landscape cannot give us except in the mountains? Something overly civilized, overly refined, overly artificial emerges from this delicate and graceful undergrowth whose ground is carpeted with little, dead leaves and quilted with spots of shade.

Another characteristic of the Antillean landscape is its force, while in France the harmony of the landscape always appears a little bit weak. To relocate force and passion and even grandeur, you have to go to the mountains, to the Gorges of Chouvigny, for example, whose river reminds me of the Martinican torrents: great, black rocks break up its course; it bubbles and foams all around without being able to cleave the obstacle, all in the frame of immense jagged boulders.

Thank God, summer's back. What a pleasure it is to get rid of those heavy furs to dress up in light fabrics with hot colors that themselves also announce the return of good weather.

This summer has come like an act of grace.

Originally published as "Actions de grâce," *La Dépêche africaine,* May 30, 1929, 3.

In Exile

Paulette Nardal

Her workday over, poor Elisa went home, clutching her black woolen shawl that replaced the fur missing from her coat. Climbing up the windy rue des Écoles, all shiny with rain, she pondered, her heart wrenched:

"This land does not truly suit an old Negress already weighed down by age and sometimes enfeebled with rheumatism."

The icy wind cut right through her thin coat. All her flesh seemed to revolt against the sensation to which she had never been able to habituate herself. Her imagination had almost personified winter, which she thought of as a cruel and implacable enemy. It came to her to wonder what fault the Europeans had committed that the good Lord had seen fit to punish them with such a scourge, for in her narrow smarts, there could be no other explanation.

"Oh! What a beautiful blond!"

Indifferent to the laughter of a bunch of students enchanted by their witty remark, she went on in her interior monologue. No, she could not keep this up much longer. This life—which left no room for contented idling, for happy and animated conversations in the evening with her roommate and her other friends, exiled like her—just seemed too painful. She would get herself repatriated as soon as possible.

What cost her the most was the frightful regularity of European life, that exactness which is the enemy of fantasy. Six o'clock in the morning. Wake up. Meticulous preparation of fragrant coffee, with punch on Sundays, her only luxury. This coffee was her triumph. She would make that veritable nectar whose recipe is known only to the Antilleans. But already she had to get dressed; and at seven o'clock, she had to take the bus to reach the dingy apartment on the rue Cuvier, where she kept house. Her old hands, despite their wrinkles and moving from hot to cold water, had maintained their native finesse, but when the cold wind blew, like this evening, she suffered cruelly from them. And despite her being bent over and the extreme fatigue she felt at night, she had been obliged to accustom herself to walking by foot all the way to the rue Racine, in order to save the piddling pennies of an extra bus stop. If only her son, who had left almost five years ago to tempt his fortune in South America, would come back to her with a little money, she would return to her homeland, to that sweet Martinique that she should never have exchanged for the mirage of Paris.

The bus was not too long in coming. The conductor, who for several weeks had enjoyed himself at her expense, had ended up taking her under his wing. He gave her a familiar smile. She found a place in second class and sat down amid a general uproar. It was especially her calendered madras, so oddly knotted, that drew glances. People didn't seem to suspect that that might bother her. To speak frankly, this particular evening, they didn't exist for her.

With a far-off gaze, she saw herself back in her birth town, Sainte-Marie, where she had spent her youth.

It's evening. After a day of ironing, she sits down on a worm-eaten bench in front of her single-story house, attracted by the chatting of friends who, like her, inhale the salt air with delight. Small talk. Enormous bursts of laughter. When the cackling stops, the sound of the sea, all glistening from moonlight, fills the silence. A funereal street lamp sparsely lights the somber and narrow street. The rays of the moon give a singular shine to the cheekbones and teeth of the talkers. They let themselves flow with the sweetness of living in the languishing atmosphere. Up above, on the hilltop, the church seems to watch over the half-asleep town, giving it a silent benediction. Someone begins to "tell tales" without forgetting to put the traditional formulas at the beginning. "Titime?," "Bois sec," "Trois fois bel conte." They are, as always, the adventures of Godfather Rabbit, of the three-legged horse. The whole Martinican folklore goes by. African tales adapted to the Antillean soul. But then the distant drum resounds. In the highlands, near Fourniolles, some *laguîa* [game] has assembled, in a clearing of trampled dirt, the rough workers from the cane fields. Two big blacks challenge each other, attack with the explosiveness of wild beasts and withdraw more light-footed than cats. As long as they don't get too excited at this dangerous game and that it's not, once more, the "laguîa of death." Another black, squatting on an overturned barrel, his straw hat pushed back, hits the stretched back of a sheepskin with expert fingers. He pulls out of it sounds that echo in the distance like an anxious call. It's the whole soul of old Africa, which passes into this Antillean tom-tom, awakening a vague emotion in the suddenly attentive talkers.

"Rue de Rennes!"

Old Elisa gives a start. That shout, the brutal lights of the storefronts, have shredded the veils of her reverie. Coming back to reality, she sees around her the strained faces, the hard eyes, the closed or indifferent physiognomies of whites. And the weight of her existence falls back more heavily on her shoulders. Her heart, too, seems heavy, heavy.

Come on. Time to get ready to get off the bus. Here is the boulevard Pasteur already. In the entryway her concierge shouts to her. "Mama Elisa, a letter for you! It's from South America!" A letter from her son! The sadness of her day is wiped away by this, and her eyes, heartbroken just before, now light up. With the nonchalance of simple people, she immediately opens the envelope, begins to read, and suddenly, suffocated with happiness, she sits down in a lounge chair. Her son, to whom the Americans have paid a good price for his skin-dressing enterprise, is returning soon to take her back home. Old Elisa weeps. This unexpected joy seems almost unbearable to her, after all those days of despair. To believe in her good fortune, she has to announce it right away to her young friend who ought to be waiting upstairs. Briskly, she climbs up her six stories, and the neighbors, who every evening have pitied her upon hearing her painfully clamber up the worn-down steps, wonder who indeed could be humming so that strange refrain with the jerky rhythm and the guttural and sweet syllables. . . .

Originally published as "En exil," *La Dépêche africaine,* December 15, 1929, 6.

The Awakening of Race Consciousness among Black Students

Paulette Nardal

I shall study this awakening more specifically among black Antilleans. Their attitude about matters of race has certainly changed. A mere few years ago, one might even say a few months, certain subjects were taboo in Martinique. Woe to those who dared broach them! One could not speak of slavery nor proclaim pride in being of African descent without being considered a fanatic or at the very least eccentric. Such matters roused no deep chord in the young or the old.

Now this quasi-contemptuous indifference seems to have transformed itself into a startled interest among the older generation and a genuine enthusiasm among the younger.

However, race consciousness among certain Antilleans had already been awakened, but it was as a result of their leaving their small native lands. The uprooting and ensuing estrangement they felt in the metropolis, where blacks have not always enjoyed such consideration as has been witnessed since the Colonial Exhibition, gave them, despite their Latin education, a Negro soul.[1] Yet this state of mind was never externalized.

The Antillean Negro's attitude regarding race, so different from that of black Americans, can easily be explained by the liberalism that characterizes French race politics vis-à-vis peoples of color. [Friedrich] Sieburg's book *Dieu est-il français?* contains, among other things, a very judicious observation on the assimilative force of the French spirit.[2] According to the German writer, the absence of color prejudice among the French is owing to their certainty of turning the Negro, in a relatively short time, into a true Frenchman. Besides, it is natural that Antilleans, products of race mixing, black and white, imbued with Latin culture, and ignorant of the history of the black race, should in the end turn toward the element that honors them the most.[3]

The situation among black Americans was quite different. Though they were not of pure racial origins either, the systematic scorn displayed by white America toward them inspired them to look for reasons, from a historical, cultural, and social point of view, for pride in the past of the black race. Consequently, race, because of the necessity to resolve the racial problem plaguing the United States since the abolition of slavery, became the core of their concerns.

It would be interesting to explore the repercussions of this situation on African American literature. As is the case with nearly all colonized people, three characteristic periods may be noted in the intellectual evolution of black Americans. First, a period of indispensable acquisitions during which the blacks imported from Africa had to learn a new language and adapt to a hostile environment. This is a period of Negro absorption. From a literary point of view, blacks could only docilely imitate the works of their white models. Only certain slave narratives retain all of their original freshness and genuine emotion thanks to the use of the African-American dialect. During the antislavery struggle, we witness the dawning of a literature of controversy and moral protest where the oratorical genre is deftly cultivated and oftentimes with success. Incessant appeals to pity characterize the poetic production then. There remain from this epoch a considerable number of documents and private papers, which, from a historical point of view, are of real value.

From 1880 onward, black Americans rose to true culture. Two opposing tendencies emerged. On one side, Dunbar, poet and novelist, who used both patois and English, represented, if we may say so, the school of racial realism. On the other, Du Bois continued, as it were, the literature of social protest by advocating civil and cultural rights for blacks equal to that of whites. But it is under the influence of Braithwaite that modern authors, starting in 1912, without abandoning Negro themes and the emotional intensity due to their ancestral sufferings, took these themes as the starting point of their inspiration and gave them universal purport. More importantly, they abandoned specifically Negro means of expression in favor of the forms and symbols of traditional literature. Our readers have had, through the verse of Claude McKay, an inkling of this new attitude. And more recently still, through the poems of Langston Hughes, they have been able to observe that the

Americans, having thrown off all inferiority complexes, tranquilly "express their individual dark-skinned selves without fear or shame."

This interesting intellectual evolution of the black American leads us to ask ourselves: Where does the Antillean, who has developed intellectually in a relatively more favorable milieu, now stand in this evolution?

If racial concerns can hardly be found in the literary productions of the period following the abolition of slavery in the Antilles, it is because our "Great Forefathers" were busy struggling for liberty and political rights for the various categories of the black race on Antillean soil.[4] From a purely literary point of view, these elders and their successors, among whom we may cite the Martinicans Victor Duquesnay, Daniel Thaly, Salavina, the Guadeloupean Oruno Lara, and many Haitian writers and poets, represent the phase of orientation toward the literature of the conquering race, which lasted until roughly 1914. But if the intellectual evolution of black Americans has been rapid, that of the black Antillean might be called prodigious. During the romantic period in Europe, the productions of Antillean writers were in no way inferior to those of French writers, not to mention such Antillean geniuses like the father and son Dumas and José Maria de Hérédia.

Needless to say, if we examine the works of these precursors, we find there the glorification of small, faraway homelands, the "Islands of Beauty" (exoticism is already in fashion), but nothing resembling race pride. Indeed, they speak lovingly of their native islands, but it so happened that a stranger celebrated them with still more blissfulness (see Lafcadio Hearn, *Esquisses martiniquaises*)[5] and showed more appreciation for and real attachment to the islands' distinct racial types. Their [Antilleans'] successors will continue to model their artistic productions after those of the metropolis.

However, between this period and the present may be classed a generation of men whose racial leanings are being channeled through literature or political and humanitarian concerns. Certain ideas are brewing. They comment on the theories of Marcus Garvey. The first Pan-Negro Congress is organized. Literature gives us *Batouala* by René Maran—who received the Prix Goncourt in 1920—a "novel of objective observation," as the author himself writes in his preface, where, nonetheless, a generous indignation stirs. Later there was the publication of the first black journal in Paris, *Les Continents,* which disappeared within a few months. We must also cite an essay "Heimatlos" written by a young man from Guyana who, during his time, had a certain success, but has since died. Then there was the creation in Paris of the first black journal of long standing, *La Dépêche africaine,* whose director, Maurice Satineau, wrote a much-appreciated history of Guadeloupe under the ancien régime. In this journal, the movement that was to culminate in *La Revue du monde noir* emerged. In the Antilles, it is important to note the remarkable works of Jules Monnerot—*Contributions à l'histoire de la Martinique*—and more recently *Les Galeries martiniquaises,* a valuable document that the author, Césaire Philémon, dedicated to his small homeland, and in which matters of race are treated with more frankness than usual.

In none of these works is the black question studied in itself, as we can plainly attest. These works remain still the tributaries of Latin culture. In none of them is expressed faith in the future of the race and the necessity to create a feeling of solidarity between the different groups of blacks disseminated throughout the globe.

However, parallel to the aforementioned isolated efforts, the aspirations that were to crystallize around *La Revue du monde noir* asserted themselves among a group of Antillean women students in Paris. The women of color living alone in the metropolis, who until the Colonial Exposition were less favored than their male compatriots, who have enjoyed easy successes, felt long before the latter the need for a racial solidarity that would not be merely material. They were thus aroused to race consciousness. The feeling of uprooting, felicitously expressed in Roberte Horth's "Histoire sans importance," published in the second issue of *La Revue du monde noir,* was the starting point of their evolution.

After having been trained obediently in the school of thought of their white models, they perhaps passed, like their black American brothers, through a period of revolt. But, with maturity, they became less severe, less intransigent, since they have understood that everything is relative. Their present position is the middle ground.

In the course of their evolution, their intellectual curiosity has turned toward the history of their race and their respective countries. They were thus led to deplore the absence of such interesting material in the educational programs implemented in the Antilles. Instead of despising their backward compatriots or losing faith in the possibility of the black race ever equaling the Aryan race, they began to study. And as a matter of course, when the occasion came to select a subject for a paper or thesis, their preference turned to that which had become the object of their concerns: the black race. For the first time, one of the female students took "The Work of Mrs. Beecher Stowe" (1. *Uncle Tom's Cabin*; 2. "Puritanism in New England") as a subject for the *diplôme d'études supérieures d'anglais*.[6] Later on, another male student of English studied Lafcadio Hearn's works on the Antilles. Still another female student of French endeavored to analyze the works of Jean Antoine-Nau and the memoirs of Father Labat. We must say that at that time, Afro-American writers were completely unknown in France. But the interest of Antillean students in their own race had begun to awaken. We have been informed that many students of English are preparing papers on Afro-American writers hitherto neglected, in spite of their evident value, in the surveys of American literature compiled by French university professors.

Let us hope that the students who are preparing for degrees in history and geography will take advantage of the riches that the past of the black race and the African continent offers them. Let us also hope that they will soon give us the occasion to analyze within the pages of this *Revue* some masterful doctoral theses. In this realm, they have had two distinguished precursors. Félix Eboué, administrator-in-chief of the colonies, has for many years studied the ethnology of certain African peoples. And there is also Grégoire Micheli, member of the International Institute of Anthropology, who has contributed remarkable articles to this *Revue,* and has devoted all his efforts to the study of the ancient religions of South America. On the other hand, we know that René Maran's new novel *Le Livre de brousse,* whose translation will appear in America, and will be in all likelihood his masterpiece, constitutes a real and splendid rehabilitation of African civilization. It is worth noting that a certain number of our young friends seem to have spontaneously arrived at the last phase that we have observed in the intellectual evolution of black Americans. If they [Antilleans] do continue to treat purely Occidental subjects, it is today in an extremely modern form and they attempt simultaneously to highlight characteristic racial themes as our readers will be able to verify in a series of interesting poems that we are soon going to publish.

Should one see in the tendencies here expressed an implicit declaration of war upon Latin culture and the white world in general? We want to eliminate such ambiguity so as to leave no doubt. We are fully conscious of our debts to Latin culture and we have no intention of discarding it in order to promote a return to I know not what obscurantism. Without it, we would have never become conscious of who we really are. But we want to go beyond this culture in order to give to our brethren, with the help of white scientists and all the friends of blacks, the pride of belonging to a race whose civilization is perhaps the oldest in the world. Once informed of that civilization, they will no longer despair of the future of their race, of which a portion seems presently lethargic. They will tender to their backward brothers a helping hand and endeavor to understand and love them better. . . .

Originally published as "L'Éveil de la conscience de race chez les étudiants noirs," *La Revue du monde noir* 6 (April 1932): 25–31.

Letter from Lieutenant de Vaisseau Bayle, Chief of Information Services, to the Editor of the Review *Tropiques*

Fort-de-France, May 10, 1943

Dear Sir,

When Madame Césaire requested from me the paper necessary for a new issue of *Tropiques,* I immediately acquiesced, seeing no objection, on the contrary, to the publication of a literary or cultural review.[1]

I do have, on the contrary, very formal objections to a revolutionary, racial, and sectarian review.

The manuscripts that have been submitted to me can leave no doubt as to these characteristics.

If you answer that this is solely a matter of a uniquely literary attitude, my response would be that everything conspires to convince the reader that this is not at all the case, and that is what counts.

Freedom? Of course, but the freedom to poison minds, to sow hatred, to destroy morals.

Let's leave aside how shocking it is to see government officials, not just paid by the French state but having achieved a high cultural level and a first-rank place in society, claim to give the signal for a revolt against a fatherland which has precisely been so very good to them. Let's also leave aside the fact that you are a professor and charged with the mission of educating young people. This in effect does not regard me directly, and let's retain only the fact that you are French.

"The Villager and the Serpent" is what would inevitably come to mind, except that you tell us that you no longer listen to "the voice of moralists, who are all policemen." Allow me to remind you, however, that this fable ends as follows: "As far as ingrates are concerned, there is not a one who doesn't die miserable."[2]

And how else but "miserable" can one conceive the fate of a society unaware of all moral rules and constraints, such as the one you are dreaming of?

Since Schoelcher, France has engaged in a politics of racial equality that it has not just proclaimed, but which it has also more sweepingly put into practice than any other country: you are living testimony of this politics, which has enjoyed the allegiance of a near majority of people of color, and many of whom have proven this allegiance by their own sacrifice.

Of course, a long way remains to go along this road. Who would deny that? Among the French there are some who have not understood this politics (which has not always been well explained to them); there are others who do not want to condone it, but they are an infinitesimal minority. Excessive centralization is an evil that has made every French province suffer. It has come close to stifling their personality, to substituting it by a conventional and uniform being, to killing art by drying up truth's wellhead. A cold, north wind is the symbol of the necessary reaction. I thought I saw in *Tropiques* the sign of a regionalism no less vigorous and every bit as desirable.

I admit that I was wrong and that you are in pursuit of a completely different objective. I think progress must be pursued by staying on the same path that has been followed for almost a century, and furthermore, I believe that the problem posed here is much more social than it is racial. It can be resolved by the kinds of principles evoked by the Maréchal [Pétain], when and if we have the courage to translate them into facts. As for you, you believe in the power of hate, of revolt, and the goal you've set is the free unleashing of every instinct, of every passion. It is a return to barbarism pure and simple. Schoelcher, whom you invoke, would be quite surprised to see his name and words used for the profit of such a cause.

It is not conceivable that a civilized State, conscious of its duties, would allow you to pursue the diffusion of such a doctrine.

I therefore forbid the publication of this issue of *Tropiques,* and I hereby return your manuscripts as an enclosure.

I beg of you, dear sir, to please accept the expression of my distinguished consideration.[3]

Signed: [Bayle]

This letter is reprinted in *Tropiques: Collection complète, 1941–1945* (Paris: Jean-Michel Place, 1978), xxxvii–xxxviii.

Response from *Tropiques*

Fort-de-France, May 12, 1943

To: Lieutenant-Commander Bayle

Dear Sir,

We are in receipt of your indictment against *Tropiques.*

"Racists," "sectarians," "revolutionaries," "ingrates and traitors to the fatherland," "poisoners of minds," none of these epithets are in essence repugnant to us.

"Poisoners of minds," like Racine, according to the gentlemen at Port-Royal.

"Ingrates and traitors to our so very good fatherland," like Zola, according to the reactionary press.

"Revolutionaries," like Victor Hugo who wrote the "Châtiments."

"Sectarians," passionately so, like Rimbaud and Lautréamont.

"Racists," yes. Racism like that of Toussaint-Louverture, Claude McKay, and Langston Hughes—against the racism like that of Drumont and Hitler.

As for the rest, expect neither pleas from us, nor recriminations, nor even debate.

We do not speak the same language.

Signed: [Aimé Césaire, Suzanne Césaire, Georges Gratiant, Aristide Maugée, René Ménil, Lucie Thésée]

This letter is reprinted in *Tropiques: Collection complète, 1941–1945* (Paris: Jean-Michel Place, 1978), xxxix.

The Malaise of a Civilization

Suzanne Césaire

If in our legends and tales we see the appearance of a suffering, sensitive, sometimes mocking being that is our collective ego, we look in vain for an expression of that ego in Martinique's ordinary literary products.

Why is it that in the past we have been so unconcerned about telling our ancestral worries directly?

The urgency of this cultural problem escapes only those who have decided to put on blinders so as not to be disturbed from an artificial tranquillity—at any price, be it that of stupidity or death.

As for us, we feel that our troubling times will bud here a ripened fruit, irresistibly called by the ardor of the sun to disperse its creative forces to the wind; we feel in this tranquil, sun-drenched land the fearsome, inexorable pressure of destiny that will dip the whole world in blood in order, tomorrow, to give it its new face.

Let us inquire into the life of this island that is ours.

What do we see?

First the geographical position of this parcel of land: tropical. In this case here, the Tropics.

Whence the adaptation here of an African settlement. The Negroes imported here had to struggle against the intense mortality of slavery in its beginnings, against the harshest work conditions ever, against chronic malnutrition—a reality that is still alive. And nevertheless, it cannot be denied that on Martinican soil the colored race produces strong, tough, supple men and women of a natural elegance and great beauty.

But, then, is it not surprising that this people, who over the centuries has adapted to this soil, this people of authentic Martinicans is just now producing authentic works of art? How is it that over the centuries no viable survivors of the original styles have been revealed—for example, those styles that have flowered so magnificently on African soil? Sculptures, ornate fabrics, paintings, poetry? Let the imbeciles reproach the race and its so-called instinct for laziness, theft, wickedness.

Let's talk seriously:

If this lack of Negroes is not explained by the hardships of the tropical climate to which we have adapted, and still less by I know not what inferiority, it is explained, I believe, as follows, by:

(1) the horrific conditions of being brutally transplanted onto a foreign soil; we have too quickly forgotten the slave ships and the sufferings of our slave fathers. Here, forgetting equals cowardice.

(2) an obligatory submission, under pain of flogging and death, to a system of "civilization," a "style" even more foreign to the new arrivals than the tropical land.

(3) finally, after the liberation of people of color, through a collective error about our true nature, an error born of the following idea, anchored in the deepest recesses of popular consciousness by centuries of suffering: "Since the superiority of the colonizers arises from a certain style of life, we can access power only by mastering the techniques of this 'style' in our turn."

Let's stop and measure the importance of this gigantic mistake.

What is the Martinican fundamentally, intimately, and inalterably? And how does he live?

In answering these questions, we will see a surprising contradiction appear between his deep being, with his desires, his impulses, his unconscious forces—and how life is lived with its necessities, its urgencies, its weight. A phenomenon of decisive importance for the future of the country.

What is the Martinican?

—A human plant.

Like a plant, abandoned to the rhythm of universal life. No effort expended to dominate nature. Mediocre at farming. Perhaps. I'm not saying he makes the plant grow; I'm saying he grows, that he lives plantlike.
His indolence? That of the vegetable kingdom. Don't say: "he's lazy," say: "he vegetates," and you will be doubly right. His favorite phrase:

"let it flow." Meaning that he lets himself flow with, be carried by life, docile, light, not insistent, not a rebel—amicably, amorously. Obstinate besides, as only a plant knows how to be. Independent (the independence and autonomy of a plant). Surrender to self, to the seasons, to the moon, to the day whether shorter or longer. The picking season. And always and everywhere, in the least of his representations, primacy of the plant, the plant that is trod upon but alive, dead but reborn, the free, silent, and proud plant.

Open your eyes—a child is born. To which god should he be confided? To the Tree god. Coconut or Banana, in whose roots they bury the placenta.

Open your ears. One of the popular tales of Martinican folklore: the grass that grows on the tomb is the living hair of the dead person, in protest to death. Always the same symbol: the plant. The lively feeling of a life-death community. In short, *the Ethiopian feeling for life.*[1]

So, the Martinican is typically Ethiopian. In the depths of his consciousness, he is the human plant, and by identifying with the plant, his desire is to surrender to life's rhythm.

Does this attitude suffice to explain his failure in the world?

No—the Martinican has failed because, misrecognizing his true nature, he tries to live a life that is not suited to him. A gigantic phenomenon of collective lying, of "pseudomorphosis." And the current state of civilization in the Caribbean reveals to us the consequences of this error.

Repression, suffering, sterility.

How, why this fatal mistake among this people enslaved until yesterday? By the most natural of processes, by the play of the survival instinct.

Remember that what the regime of slavery above all forbade was the *assimilation of the Negro to the white.* Some choice ordinances: that of April 30, 1764, which forbids blacks and coloreds from practicing medicine; that of May 9, 1765, which forbids them from working as notary publics; and the famous ordinance of February 9, 1779, which formally forbids blacks from wearing the same clothes as whites, demands respect for and submission to "all whites in general," etc., etc.

Let's cite too the ordinance of January 3, 1788, which obliged free men of color "to request a permit if they wished to work *anywhere but in cultivation.*" It is understood henceforth that the essential goal for the colored man has become that of *assimilation.* And with a fearsome force, the disastrous conclusion forms in his head: *liberation equals assimilation.*

In the beginning, the movement was off to a good start: 1848; the masses of freed blacks, in a sudden explosion of primitive ego, incorrectly renounced all regular work, despite the danger of famine. But the Negroes, subdued by economics, no longer slaves but wage earners, submitted once more to the discipline of the hoe and the cutlass.

And this is the era that definitively establishes the repression of the ancestral desire for letting go.

That desire is replaced, especially in the colored bourgeoisie, by the foreign desire of struggle.

Whence the drama, evident to those who analyze in depth the collective ego of the Martinican people: their unconscious continues to be inhabited by the Ethiopian desire for letting go. But their consciousness, or rather their preconsciousness, accepts the Hamitic desire for struggle. The race to riches. To diplomas. Ambition. Struggle reduced to the level of the bourgeoisie. The race to monkey-like imitations. Vanity fair.

The most serious consequence is that the desire to imitate, which had formally been vaguely conscious—since it was a defense reaction against an oppressive society—now passed into the ranks of the fearsome, secret forces of the unconscious.

No "evolved" Martinican would accept that he is only imitating, so much does his current situation appear natural, spontaneous, born of his most legitimate aspirations. And, in so doing, he would be sincere. He truly does not KNOW that he is imitating. He is *unaware* of his true nature, which does not cease to exist for that matter.

Just as the *hysteric* is unaware that he is merely *imitating* an illness, but the doctor, who cares for him and delivers him from his morbid symptoms, knows it.

Likewise, analysis shows us that the effort to adapt to a foreign style that is demanded of the Martinican does not take place without creating a state of pseudocivilization that can be qualified as *abnormal, teratoid.*

The problem today is to determine if the Ethiopian attitude we discovered as the very essence of the Martinican's feeling for life can be the point of departure for a viable, hence imposing, cultural style.

It is exalting to imagine in these tropical lands, finally rendered to their internal truth, the long-lasting and fruitful accord between man and soil. Under the sign of the plant.

Here we are called upon finally to know ourselves, and here before us stand splendor and hope. Surrealism gave us back some of our possibilities. It is up to us to find the rest. By its guiding light.

Understand me well:

It is not a question of a return to the past, of resurrecting an African past that we have learned to appreciate and respect. On the contrary, it is a question of mobilizing every living force mingled together on this land where race is the result of the most continuous brazing; it is a question of becoming conscious of the tremendous heap of various energies we have until now locked up within ourselves. We must now put them to use in their fullness, without deviation and without falsification. Too bad for those who thought we were idle dreamers.

The most troubling reality is our own.

We shall act.

This land, our land, can only be what we want it to be.

Originally published as "Malaise d'une civilisation," *Tropiques* 5 (April 1942): 43–49.

The Great Camouflage

Suzanne Césaire

There are, layered up against the islands, the beautiful green waves of water and silence. There is the purity of salt in and about the Antilles. There is before my eyes the pretty Place de Pétionville, planted with pines and hibiscus. There is my island, Martinique, and its fresh necklace of clouds puffed up by Mount Pelée. There are the highest plateaus of Haiti, where a horse dies, lightning-struck by the secularly murderous storm at Hinche. Nearby, his master contemplates the country he thought to be solid and expansive. He doesn't yet know that he is participating in the islands' lack of equilibrium. But this stroke of terrestrial insanity enlightens his heart: he begins to think about the other Antilles, about their volcanoes, their earthquakes, their hurricanes.

At this moment off the coast of Puerto Rico a great cyclone begins to turn amid seas of clouds, with its beautiful tail that rhythmically sweeps the half circle of the Caribbean isles. The Atlantic flees toward Europe in great oceanic waves. Our little tropical observatories begin to crackle with the news. The wireless goes haywire. Boats flee, flee where? The sea swells, here and there an exertion, a delectable surge, the water slackens its limbs to get a wider consciousness of its watery power, sailors with clenched teeth and a streaming face, and we learn that the southeast coast of Haiti is under the cyclone that passes at twenty-five miles per hour, heading toward Florida. Consternation takes hold of the objects and beings spared from the wind by being at its fringe. Don't move. Let it pass. . . .

In the heart of the cyclone, everything crackles, everything crumbles with the ripping sound of great displays. Then the radios fall silent. The great tail of palms of cool wind is unfurled somewhere in the stratosphere, there where no one will follow the crazy iridescences and violet lightwaves.

After the rain, then sun.

Haitian cicadas think about grinding love. When there is not a single drop of water left in the burnt grass, they sing furiously that life is beautiful, they burst out in a cry that is too vibrant for an insect body. Their thin pellicle of dried silk stretched to the extreme, they die suffusing the least moist cry of pleasure in the world.

Haiti remains, wrapped in the embers of the sun that are sweet to the eyes of the cicadas, to the scales of the *mabouyas,* to the metal face of the sea which is no longer made of water but of mercury.[1]

Now is the time to lean out the window of the aluminum clipper with its great turns.

The airplanes of the Pan American Airways System pass through once again the no-longer-virgin sea of clouds. If there is a harvest ripening, that is the time to try to get a glimpse of it [Haiti], but in the closed-off military zones, the windows are closed.

They bring out disinfectants, or ozone, it doesn't matter, you will see nothing. Nothing but the sea and the dim form of lands. We can only guess about the easy love of fish. They make the water move, which amicably winks at the clipper's porthole. Viewed from very high up, our islands take on their true dimension as shells. And as for the hummingbird-women, the tropical flower–women, the women of four races and dozens of bloodlines, they are no longer there. Neither the canna, nor the plumeria and the flame trees, neither the palms by moonlight, nor the sunsets unlike any other in the world . . .

Nevertheless, they are there.

Nevertheless, fifteen years ago, the Antilles were revealed to me from the flank of Mount Pelée. From here I discovered, though still very young, that Martinique was sensual, coiled up, extended, distended into the Caribbean Sea, and I thought about the other islands that are so beautiful.

Once again in Haiti, during the summer mornings of 1944, I experienced the presence of the Antilles, more perceptible in places from which, like at Kenscoff, the mountain views are of an unbearable beauty.

And now, total lucidity. Beyond these perfect colors and forms, my gaze detects the innermost torments in the Antilles' most beautiful face.

For the plot of unsatisfied desires has ensnared the Antilles and

America. Since the arrival of the conquistadors and the maturation of their technology (beginning with that of firearms), the ultra-Atlantic lands have not only changed face, but also fear. Fear of being outpaced by those who remained in Europe, already armed and appointed, the fear of being in competition with peoples of color that were hurriedly pronounced inferior so as the better to torment them. It was necessary at first and at all costs, be it the cost of the slave trade's infamy, to create an American society richer, more powerful, and better organized than the European society left behind—and desired. It was necessary to take this revenge upon the nostalgic hell that belched forth its adventurous demons, its convicts, its penitents, and its utopians upon the New World and its islands. After three centuries, the colonial adventure continues—the wars of independence are but an episode—the peoples of the Americas, whose behavior toward the peoples of Europe remains often infantile and romantic, are still not free of the old continent's ascendancy. Naturally, the blacks in America are those who suffer the most, in a day-by-day humiliation, from the degeneracies, injustices, and pettiness of colonial society.

If we are proud to note our extraordinary vitality everywhere in the Americas, if that vitality seems definitively to promise our salvation, nonetheless it must dare be said that refined forms of slavery continue to be rife. Here, in the French islands, they debase thousands of blacks for whom the great Schoelcher sought, a century ago, along with freedom and dignity, the title of citizen. It must dare be shown, on the face of France, lit by the implacable light of events, the Antillean stain, since there are also indeed many among the French who seem determined to tolerate no shadow upon that face.

The degrading forms of modern wage labor still find among us a ground upon which to flourish without constraint.

Who will throw out, along with the antiquated material of their factories, these few thousand submanufacturers and shopkeepers, that caste of false colonizers responsible for the human deprivation of the Antilles?

When they are left off on the streets of their capitals, an insurmountable timidity fills them with fear among their European brethren. Ashamed of their drawling accent, of their unsure French, they sigh after the tranquil warmth of Antillean dwellings and the patois of the black "nanny" of their childhood.

Ready to betray any and all in order to defend themselves against the rising tide of blacks, they would sell themselves to America were it not that the Americans claim that the purity of their blood is highly suspect,[2] just as in the 1940s they devoted themselves to the Admiral of Vichy: Pétain being for them the altar of France, Robert necessarily became "the tabernacle of the Antilles."

In the meantime, the Antillean serf lives with misery and abjection on the grounds of the "factory," and the mediocre state of our cities-towns is a nauseating spectacle. In the meantime, the Antilles continue to be like paradise and that sweet sound of palms. . . .

That day the irony was that, a shiny garment full of sparkles, each of our muscles expressed in a personal manner one parcel of the desire scattered among the blossoming mango trees.

I listened very attentively without being able to hear your voices lost in the Caribbean symphony that would hurl waterspouts against the islands. We were just like thoroughbreds, held back, impatiently pawing the ground, at the edge of that salt savanna.

On the beach, there were several "metropolitan officials." They were installed there, without conviction, and ready to take off at the first signal. The newcomers can scarcely adapt to our "old French lands." When they look into the maleficent mirror of the Caribbean, they see a delirious image of themselves. They dare not recognize themselves in that ambiguous being: the Antillean. They know that the métis share some of their blood, that they are also, like them, part of Western civilization. It is well understood that the "metropolitans" don't know racial prejudice. But their colored descendants fill them with dread, despite the exchange of smiles. They did not expect that strange burgeoning of their blood. Perhaps they didn't want to answer the Antillean heir who does and does not cry out "my father." However, these unexpected sons, these charming daughters must be reckoned with. These turbulent folks must be governed.

Here is an Antillean, the great-grandson of a colonist and a black slave woman. Here he is on his island, seeing to its "running" in deploying all the energies once necessary for the greedy colonists, for whom other people's blood was the natural price of gold, and all the courage necessary for African warriors who forever gained their life through death.

Here he is with his double force and double ferociousness, in a dangerous equilibrium: he cannot accept his Negritude, yet he cannot make himself become white. Listlessness overtakes this heart divided in two, and with it comes the habit of rusing, the taste for "schemes." So blossoms in the Antilles that flower of human baseness, the colored bourgeoisie.

Along the roads bordered with glyciridia, pretty little Negro children ecstatically digesting their roots cooked either with or without salt smile at the luxury automobile passing by. They suddenly feel, planted in their navel, the need to be, one day, masters of an equally supple, shiny, and powerful beast. Years later you see them, sullied with the fat of happiness, miraculously give the tremor of life to junkyard carcasses, sold for a low price. Instinctively, the hands of thousands of young Antilleans have felt the weight of steel, have located joints, unscrewed bolts. Thousands of images of brightly lit factories, virgin steel, of liberating machines, have swollen the hearts of our young laborers. In hundreds of sordid sheds where scrap metal rusts away, there is an invisible vegetation of desire. The impatient fruits of the Revolution will inevitably spring forth from this.

Here among the bluffs polished by the wind, the free-person's estate. A peasant who himself has not been swept up by the uproar of mechanical adventure leans up against the big *mapou* that gives shade to an entire flank of the bluff, and he feels grow in him, through his naked toes sunken in the mud, a slow vegetal growth.[3] He has turned toward the sunset to know what the weather will be like tomorrow—the orange reds show him that planting time is near—not only is his gaze the peaceful reflection of the light, but he grows heavy with impatience, the very impatience that uplifts the land of Martinique—his land that does not belong to him and *is* nonetheless his land. He knows that it is the workers with whom he has common cause, and not with the *béké* or the *métis*. And when, suddenly, in the middle of the Caribbean night all decked out with love and silence, a drum call bursts out, the blacks get ready to answer the desire of the earth and of the dance, but the owners lock themselves up in their beautiful houses, and behind their wire gauze, beneath the electrical light, they are just like pale butterflies caught in a snare.

All around them, the tropical night swells with rhythms, the hips of Bergilde have taken their cataclysmic allure from the swells pushed up from the depths to the sides of volcanoes. And it is Africa itself which, across the Atlantic and across the centuries before slave ships, dedicates to its Antillean children the lustfully solar glances exchanged between dancers. With a raw and wide voice, their cry exclaims that Africa is there, present, that she waits, immensely virginal despite the colonization, turbulent, devourer of whites. And upon these faces constantly bathed by the marine exhalations close to the islands, upon these limited and tiny lands surrounded by water like so many great, impassable moats, there passes an enormous wind come from Africa. Antilles-Africa, thanks to the drums, the nostalgia for terrestrial spaces, lives in these hearts of the insular. Who will fulfill that nostalgia?

Meanwhile, the cannas of Absalom bleed over chasms, and the beauty of the tropical landscape goes to the head of the poets who pass by. Across the shifting networks of palms they see the Antillean conflagration roll onto the Caribbean, which is a peaceful sea of lava. Here, life is lit by a vegetal fire. Here, on these hot lands that keep geological species alive, is found the fixed plant, passion and blood, in its primitive architecture, the anxious ringing emerging from the chaotic backs of the dancers. Here, the creepers swinging vertiginously take on airy allures to charm the precipices; with their trembling hands they hook on to the ungraspable cosmic tremor that rises all through the nights inhabited by drums. Here, the poets feel their heads overturn, and inhaling the fresh scents of the ravines, they take hold of the islands in their spread, they listen to the noise of the water around the islands, they see the tropical flames flare up no longer on account of cannas, gerberas, hibiscuses, bougainvilleas, or flame trees, but on account of the hungers, fears, hatreds, and ferocity that burn in the hollows of hills.

So it is that the conflagration of the Caribbean puffs out its silent vapors, blinding for the only eyes able to see, and suddenly the blues of the Haitian bluffs grow dim, suddenly the most dazzling reds grow pale, and the sun is no longer a crystal that plays, and if the public places have chosen Jerusalem thorns as their deluxe fans against the heat of the sky, if the flowers have found the right colors to make one thunderstruck, if the tree ferns have secreted a golden sap from their crook, all coiled up like a sex organ, if my Antilles are so beautiful, then it's because the great game of hide-and-seek has succeeded, and certainly that day would be too enchanting for us to see.

Originally published as "Le Grand camouflage," *Tropiques* 13–14 (September 1945): 267–73.

Notes

Unless otherwise noted, all translations are my own.

INTRODUCTION

1. Janet Vaillant, *Black, French, and African: A Life of Léopold Sédar Senghor* (Cambridge: Harvard University Press, 1990), 1.

2. Georges Ngal, *Lire "Le Discours sur le colonialisme"* (Paris: Présence Africaine, 1994), 13.

3. Léon Damas made this claim in "From René Maran to Negritude," in *Critical Perspectives on Léon-Gontran Damas,* ed. Keith Q. Warner (Boulder, Colo.: Three Continents, 1988), 22. This essay originally appeared as a preface to *Voix françaises du monde noir,* comp. Keith Q. Warner (New York: Holt, Rinehart & Winston, 1971), ix–x.

4. Léon Damas, "La Négritude en question," in *Critical Perspectives,* 13. This essay originally appeared in *Jeune Afrique,* no. 532 (16 March 1971).

5. Unlike *Negritude, nègreries* is not a Césairean neologism. The word was used in the section of the newspaper *La Dépêche africaine* (1928–1932) titled "Ce qu'on pense de nous." "Of Things Negro" is an attempt to translate the spirit of the word.

6. Aimé Césaire, "Nègreries: Jeunesse noire et assimilation," *L'Étudiant noir: Journal de l'Association des étudiants martiniquais en France* 1 (March 1935): 3.

7. Although "race" today is generally recognized as a social construction having no biological legitimacy, Negritude depended on the idea of a black sensibility, a black essence. Throughout the text, the author thus does not put *race* in quotation marks, for its existence was accepted and the material conditions of Antilleans attested to its ability to circumscribe their situations.

8. A. Césaire, "Nègreries," 3.

9. Léopold Sédar Senghor, "L'Humanisme et nous: René Maran," *L'Étudiant noir* 1 (March 1935): 4.

10. Léopold Sédar Senghor, *Liberté 1: Négritude et humanisme* (Paris: Seuil, 1964), 24.

11. Paulette Nardal, "Guignol ouolof," *L'Étudiant noir* 1 (March 1935): 4.

12. Gilbert Gratiant, "Mulâtres . . . pour le bien et pour le mal," *L'Étudiant noir* 1 (March 1935): 7.

13. The Negritude writers understood culture as being "made up of a determined set of living conditions (land, race, economic forms, etc.), which is mitigated by all the contingencies of everyday life that are concretely lived by the human individual." See René Ménil's "Naissance de notre art," *Tropiques* 1 (April 1941): 55.

14. Vaillant, *Black, French, and African,* 90.

15. Ibid., 91.

16. The interviews were originally published in Lilyan Kesteloot, *Les Écrivains noirs de langue française: Naissance d'une littérature* (Brussels: Éditions de l'Institut de Sociologie de l'Université Libre de Bruxelles, 1963); however, all citations throughout *Negritude Women* are from Ellen Conroy Kennedy's translation, titled *Black Writers in French: A Literary History of Negritude* (Washington, D.C.: Howard University Press, 1991), 119–20.

17. Léopold Sédar Senghor, ed., *Anthologie de la nouvelle poésie nègre et malgache de langue française* (Paris: Presses Universitaire de France, 1948), 5.

18. Léon Damas, "Trève," in *Pigments* (Paris: Présence Africaine Éditions, 1962), 21.

19. Frantz Fanon, *Black Skin, White Masks* (originally published as *Peau noire, masques blancs*), trans. Charles Lam Markmann (New York: Grove, 1967), 173.

20. Damas, "Solde," in *Pigments,* 39–40.

21. Damas, "Limbé," in *Pigments,* 42.

22. Aimé Césaire, *Cahier d'un retour au pays natal/Return to My Native Land,* bilingual ed. (Paris: Présence Africaine Éditions, 1971), 72/73.

23. Fanon, *Black Skin, White Masks,* 12.

24. Frantz Fanon, *The Wretched of the Earth,* trans. Constance Farrington (New York: Grove, 1965), 41.

25. A. Césaire, *Cahier/Return,* 128/129.

26. Michael Seidel, *Exile and the Narrative Imagination* (New Haven: Yale University Press, 1986), ix.

27. Léopold Sédar Senghor, "Prière de paix," in *Hosties noires* (Paris: Seuil, 1964), 92–98. The version quoted here is from "Peace Prayer," in *The Collected Poetry,* trans. Melvin Dixon (Charlottesville: University Press of Virginia, 1991), 69–71.

28. See Senghor, *Liberté 1,* 316. In a lecture delivered at the Sorbonne in 1961, Senghor says: "Jean-Paul Sartre n'a pas tout à fait raison quand, dans 'Orphée noir,' il définit la Négritude 'un racisme antiracisme'" [Jean-Paul

Sartre was not at all correct, when in "Black Orpheus," he defined Negritude as "an antiracist racism"].

29. Damas, "La Négritude en question," 13: Damas stated in an interview with *Jeune Afrique,* "Our purpose devoid of any trace of racism was to turn to ourselves."

30. Jean-Paul Sartre, "Black Orpheus," in *"What Is Literature?" and Other Essays* (Cambridge: Harvard University Press, 1988), 296.

31. Léopold Sédar Senghor, qtd. in Jacques Louis Hymans, *Léopold Sédar Senghor: An Intellectual Biography* (Edinburgh: Edinburgh University Press, 1971), 71.

32. See Michael Richardson, ed., *Refusal of the Shadow: Surrealism and the Caribbean,* trans. Krzysztof Fijalkowski and Michael Richardson (London: Verso, 1996), 6–8.

33. René Ménil, "Une doctrine réactionnaire: La négritude," *Action: Revue théorique et politique du Parti communiste martiniquais* 1 (August 1963): 37–40.

34. Marcien Towa, *Léopold Sédar Senghor: Négritude ou servitude?* (Yaoundé, Cameroon: Éditions Clé, 1971), 99.

35. Qtd. in René Ménil's *Tracées: Identité, négritude, esthètique aux Antilles* (Paris: Robert Laffont, 1985), 27. The original statement by de Gaulle was, "Entre Amérique et l'Europe, il n'y a que l'Océan and quelques poussières!"

36. Jean Verdier, introduction to *L'Homme de couleur* (Paris: Plon, 1939), xi.

37. The Surrealist Group in Paris, "Murderous Humanitarianism," in *Negro: An Anthology,* ed. Nancy Cunard (New York: Continuum, 1996), 353.

38. Léon Damas, *Retour de Guyane* (Paris: Corti, 1938), 168.

39. Léopold Sédar Senghor, "Ce que l'homme noir apporte," in Verdier, *L'Homme de couleur,* 292–314.

40. René Ménil, "De la négritude," in *Tracées*; and "Une doctrine reactionnaire."

41. Fanon, *Black Skin, White Masks,* 14. In his essay "On National Culture," in *The Wretched of the Earth,* Fanon also challenged these "men of culture" to engage with the culture of the day and leveled a subtle critique of Léopold Senghor after the 1959 Black Writers and Artists Conference in Rome in a footnote of that essay.

42. Jean Bernabé, Patrick Chamoiseau, and Raphaël Confiant, *Éloge de la créolité/In Praise of Creoleness,* bilingual ed. (Paris: Gallimard, 1993), 79–80.

43. Léopold Sédar Senghor, "Problematique de la négritude," *Présence africaine* 78 (1971): 12–14.

44. René Maran, *Batouala: Véritable roman nègre* (Paris: Albin Michel, 1921), 11.

45. Senghor, "L'Humanisme et nous," 4; see Maran's novel *Un homme pareil aux autres* (Paris: Éditions Arc-en-ciel, 1947).

46. *La Dépeche coloniale,* December 26, 1921; cited also in Kesteloot, *Black Writers in French,* 75.

47. See Philippe Dewitte's excellent study *Les Mouvements nègres en France, 1919–1939* (Paris: L'Harmattan, 1985), specifically pp. 40–43 and 68–70 on René Maran.

48. Maran, *Batouala*, 11–13, 15.

49. Kesteloot, *Black Writers in French*, 75. Kesteloot interviewed Maran in March 1959.

50. Damas, "From René Maran to Negritude," 21–22; Léopold Sédar Senghor, "René Maran, précurseur de la négritude," in *Liberté 1*, 407–11.

51. D. A. Masolo's fascinating study *African Philosophy in Search of Identity* (Bloomington: Indiana University Press, 1994) briefly mentions the Nardals. There are other exceptions as well, such as Clarisse Zimra's "Négritude in the Feminine Mode: The Case of Martinique and Guadeloupe," *Journal of Ethnic Studies* 12, no. 1 (1984): 53–77; Belinda Jack's *Negritude and Literary Criticism: The History and Theory of "Negro-African" Literature in French* (Westport, Conn.: Greenwood, 1996); Michel Fabre's *From Harlem to Paris: Black American Writers in France, 1840–1980* (Urbana: University of Illinois Press, 1991); and Philippe Dewitte's *Les Mouvements nègres en France*. Most of these works briefly mention the Nardals or refer to them as "proto-Negritude" writers.

52. Maryse Condé seems to be the first and only critic and writer so far to venture to recover Lacascade, in her book-length literary essay *Parole des femmes: Essai sur les romancières des Antilles de langue française* (Paris: L'Harmattan, 1993) and in her article "Language and Power: Words as Miraculous Weapons," *CLA Journal* 39, no. 1 (1995): 18–25.

53. Suzanne Lacascade, *Claire-Solange, âme africaine* (Paris: E. Figuière, 1924).

54. Maryse Condé, "Order, Disorder, Freedom, and the West Indian Writer," *Yale French Studies* 83 (1994): 131.

55. See Carolyn J. Mooney, "On Martinique, Elevating the Status of Creole," *Chronicle of Higher Education*, June 9, 2000, B2. See also Frantz Fanon's discussion of the Creole language in "The Negro and Language," in *Black Skin, White Masks*.

56. See Damas, *Pigments*; and "Entretien avec Aimé Césaire par Jacqueline Leiner," in *Tropiques: Collection complète, 1941–1945* (Paris: Jean-Michel Place, 1978). Ronnie Scharfman presents an interesting argument with respect to Césaire's position on the Creole language. According to Scharfmann, "[T]he revalorization of an autochthonous language risks not only being reactionary but also being condemned to remain within the confines of the colonial dialectic. . . . Creole is not the proud survivor of a once-glorious past as is Arabic or native African languages. On the contrary, it bears the mark of the master's branding iron. It is the impoverished, adulterated reflection of a more recent past, its mere existence and derivative make-up bearing witness to the cultural dissipation and castration effected by slavery. This, of course, does not signify that it is completely devoid of its own history, folklore, or affect. It only means

that its scope is so circumscribed that its revival has never been an option for Césaire, though it has been for others. Césaire's position is therefore paradigmatic, absolute." Scharfman, *Engagement and the Language of the Subject in the Poetry of Aimé Césaire* (Gainesville: University of Florida Press, 1980), 13.

57. Mayotte Capécia, *Je suis Martiniquaise* (Paris: Corrêa, 1948).

58. *Grand Larousse de la langue française* (1972), s.v. "Creole." *Creole* was often used to differentiate New World blacks, that is, blacks born in the New World, from Africans newly imported to the colonies.

59. The three future Negritude poets also received inspiration from the French romantics Arthur Rimbaud and Charles Baudelaire and used as tools of critical engagement Leo Frobenius's and Maurice Delafosse's ethnology. André Breton's surrealism, particularly with respect to *Tropiques,* would not play a pivotal role until the 1940s.

60. Senghor, qtd. in Kesteloot, *Black Writers in French,* 56. Kesteloot obtained this quotation from a February 1960 letter written by Senghor.

61. Paulette Nardal, qtd. in Hymans, *Léopold Sédar Senghor,* 36.

62. As late as the 1980s, Aimé Césaire finally claimed Paulette Nardal as an "initiatrice" of the movement and named a square in Fort-de-France in her honor.

63. See, for instance, Jane Nardal, "Le Soir tombe sur Karukera," in *La Revue du monde noir* 4 (February 1932): 42–43.

64. See the "Our Next Issue" contents of *La Revue du monde noir* 5 (March 1932). Also see Hymans, *Léopold Sédar Senghor,* 38–47.

65. See Hymans, *Léopold Sédar Senghor,* 42.

66. Paulette Nardal, "Actions de grâces," *La Dépêche africaine,* May 30, 1929, 3. See the appendix for the complete translated text.

67. Paulette Nardal, "En exil," *La Dépêche africaine,* December 15, 1929, 6. See the translation in the appendix.

68. Paulette Nardal, "L'Éveil de la conscience de race chez les étudiants noirs," *La Revue du monde noir* 6 (April 1932): 25–31. See the appendix for an edited retranslation of this essay.

69. Maryse Condé, "Unheard Voice: Suzanne Césaire and the Construct of a Caribbean Identity," in *Winds of Change: The Transforming Voices of Caribbean Women Writers and Scholars,* ed. Adele Newson and Linda Strong-Leek (New York: Peter Lang, 1998), 62.

70. Richardson, *Refusal of Shadow,* 7.

71. Suzanne Césaire, "1943: Le Surréalisme et nous," *Tropiques* 8–9 (October 1943): 18.

72. There is some mystery as to Suzanne Lacascade's origins. Because she married a Guadeloupean, some literary historians assume she was Guadeloupean.

73. Zimra, "Négritude in the Feminine Mode," 62.

74. René Ménil, preface to *Légitime défense: Collection complète* (Paris: Jean-Michel Place, 1979), n.p.

75. William Shakespeare, *The Tempest*, Harvard Classics, ed. Charles W. Eliot (Danbury, Conn.: Grolier, 1980).

76. Condé, "Language and Power," 19.

I. RACE SIGNS OF THE INTERWAR TIMES

1. "Notre But—Notre Programme," *La Dépêche africaine*, February 15, 1928, 1.

2. As a sign of respect in French, strangers and even acquaintances use "vous" to address one another. Thus, addressing the Antilleans in "tu," particularly since they were from the educated social class, was a sign of disrespect. Rather than social leveling, it represented contempt, an inferiorization of the Antilleans as not French and thus as undeserving of the French formality. See Philippe Dewitte, *Les Mouvements nègres en France, 1919–1939* (Paris: L'Harmattan, 1985), 53.

3. See Michel Fabre, *From Harlem to Paris: Black American Writers in France, 1840–1980* (Urbana: University of Illinois Press, 1991); Dewitte, *Les Mouvements nègres en France*; Imanuel Geiss, *The Pan-African Movement: A History of Pan-Africanism in American, Europe, and Africa* (New York: African Publishing, 1974); and Clarence Contee, "Du Bois, the NAACP, and the Pan-African Congress of 1919," *Journal of Negro History* 57, no. 1 (January 1972): 13–28.

4. W. E. B. Du Bois, *The Souls of Black Folk: Essays and Sketches* (New York: Fawcett, 1961).

5. See Janet Vaillant, *Black, French, and African: A Life of Léopold Sédar Senghor* (Cambridge: Harvard University Press, 1990), 46.

6. David Levering Lewis, *W. E. B. Du Bois*, vol. 1, *Biography of a Race, 1868–1919* (New York: Holt, 1993), 566–67.

7. See the Archives d'outre mer in Aix-en-Provence (ADO), Slotfom (Service de liaison des originaires des territoires française d'outre mer) III, 81, no. 562, October 20, 1928, and no. 595, November 9, 1928.

8. Lewis, *W. E. B. Du Bois*, 566.

9. "Notre But—Notre Programme," 1.

10. Addie Hunton and Kathryn Johnson, *Two Colored Women with the American Expeditionary Forces* (New York: Hall, 1997), 253–54.

11. See Tyler Stovall's *Paris Noir: African Americans in the City of Light* (Boston: Houghton Mifflin, 1996) for more on the reception of African Americans in France during the interwar period.

12. W. E. B. Du Bois, "Negro at Paris," in *Writings by W. E. B. Du Bois in Periodicals Edited by Others*, vol. 2, *1910–1934*, ed. Herbert Aptheker (Millwood, N.Y.: Kraus-Thomson Organization, 1982), 127–29.

13. See Maurice Delafosse, "Le Congrès panafricain," *Bulletin du Comité de l'Afrique françaises* (March–April 1919): 53–59. See also Geiss, *The Pan-African Movement*; and Lewis, *W. E. B. Du Bois*, 574–78.

14. ADO, Slotfom III, 29, "Association pan-africaine et congrès," November 10, 1921, as signed by André Maginot. The conference of 1900 in London took place in July, not August as Maginot mistakenly notes.

15. ADO, Slotfom III, 29, "Association pan-africaine et congrès," as detailed in a handwritten report by Agent Désiré in July 1923.

16. René Maran, "La France et ses nègres," *L'Action coloniale,* September 25, 1923, 1.

17. Dewitte, *Les Mouvements nègres en France,* 59. Michel Fabre also mentions the growing tensions between Diagne and Du Bois in *From Harlem to Paris,* 59.

18. ADO, Slotfom III, 29, as reported by Agent Désiré in July 1923.

19. W. E. B. Du Bois, "The Pan-African Movement," in *History of the Pan-African Congress,* ed. George Padmore (Manchester, England: Pan-African Federation, n.d.), 18.

20. ADO, Slotfom III, 81, no. 595, as reported by Agent Désiré on November 9, 1928.

21. The government revoked the license of the proprietor. For more on the Tovalou racial incident, see *L'Action coloniale,* August 25, 1923.

22. Kojo Tovalou, "Paris coeur de la race noire," *Les Continents,* October 1, 1924.

23. *La Dépêche africaine* stopped publication for the first time in 1932. The journal then resumed publication in 1938 for one year before it eventually folded for good.

24. "Une bonne nouvelle," *La Dépêche africaine,* November 15, 1928, 2.

25. ADO, Slotfom V, 2, *"La Dépêche africaine,"* November 29, 1928.

26. *La Dépêche africaine,* January 15, 1929, publicity page.

27. *La Dépêche africaine,* May 30, 1929, 3.

28. See ADO, Slotfom V, 2, *"La Dépêche africaine* et reports policiers," May 30, 1930.

29. "Notre But—Notre Programme," 1.

30. Maurice Satineau, "Le Schoelcherisme: Doctrine politique, economique, et sociale," *La Dépêche africaine,* February 15, 1932, 1.

31. Robert Wibaux, "Elites noires," *La Dépêche africaine,* April 15, 1929, 1.

32. Union fédérale des étudiants, "Aux étudiants des colonies françaises," *La Dépêche africaine,* November 15, 1928, 6.

33. "Un suprême appel au président Hoover: L'Exécution des sept nègres serait un crime contre l'humanité," *La Dépêche africaine,* April 1, 1932, 1.

34. ADO, Slotfom III, 81, no. 595. The original report reads: "C'est addresse et ce numéro de téléphone sont presentement ceux de la direction du journal 'La Dépêche africaine.' Il n'est donc plus possible de nier les relations qui unissent cette feuille et l'organization pan-noire. Ceci explique pourquoi, ainsi qui nous le signalions dans la note du Fevrier dernier page 10, 'La Dépêche africaine' a evoqué le souvenir du defunt organ pan-noir 'les Continents.'"

35. ADO, Slotfom III, 81, no. 678, December 18, 1928.

36. ADO, Slotfom III, 81, no. 595, November 9, 1928.

37. ADO, Slotfom III, 81, no. 678, December 18, 1928: "Le numéro 9 de la 'Dépêche africaine' a paru le 15 Novembre. Le camouflage persiste: le portrait du nouveau ministre des colonies est publié en premier page avec de commentaire sympathique."

38. Alain Locke, ed., *The New Negro* (New York: Atheneum, 1969).

39. "La Dépêche littéraire," *La Dépêche africaine,* June 15, 1928, 4.

40. Paulette Nardal, "En exil," *La Dépêche africaine,* December 15, 1929, 6 (see the complete translation in the appendix); "Musique nègre: Antilles et AfraAmérique," *La Dépêche africaine,* June 30, 1930, 5; "Une femme sculpteur noire," *La Dépêche africaine,* August–September 30, 1930, 5.

41. See Fabre, *From Harlem to Paris;* and Dewitte, *Les Mouvements nègres en France,* 251–67.

2. JANE NARDAL

1. Karukera is the Caribbean name for Guadeloupe.

2. Archives d'outre mer in Aix-en-Provence, Slotfom (Service de liaison des originaires des territoires française d'outre mer) III, 81, no. 132, March 13, 1928.

3. W. E. B. Du Bois, "Negro at Paris," in *Writings by W. E. B. Du Bois in Periodicals Edited by Others,* vol. 2, *1910–1934,* ed. Herbert Aptheker (Millwood, N.Y.: Kraus-Thomson Organizations, 1982), 127.

4. Jane Nardal, "Internationalisme noir," *La Dépêche africaine,* February 15, 1928, 5. See the appendix for the complete translated text.

5. Alain Locke, ed., *The New Negro* (New York: Atheneum, 1969), xvii.

6. W. E. B. Du Bois, *The Souls of Black Folk: Essays and Sketches* (New York: Fawcett, 1961), 17.

7. J. Nardal, "Internationalisme noir," 5.

8. Raoul Girardet, *Le Nationalisme français: Anthologie, 1871–1914* (Paris: Seuil, 1983), 86.

9. Frantz Fanon, *A Dying Colonialism,* trans. Haakon Chevalier (New York: Grove, 1965), 63.

10. Jules Michelet, *L'Introduction à l'histoire universelle* (Paris: Librairie Armand Colin, 1962), 64.

11. Girardet, *Le Nationalisme français,* 86.

12. See Jacques Louis Hymans, *Léopold Sédar Senghor: An Intellectual Biography* (Edinburgh: Edinburgh University Press, 1971). In Senghor's correspondence with Paulette Nardal, she proclaims what her and Jane's intentions were and were not.

13. "La Trahison du clerc Paul Morand," *La Race nègre,* October 1928, 2.

14. Paul Morand, *Black Magic* (originally published as *Magie noire*), trans. Hamish Miles (New York: Viking, 1929), 150.

15. Jane Nardal, "Pantins exotiques," *La Dépêche africaine,* October 15, 1928, 2. See the appendix for the complete translated text.

16. Ibid. *Capresse* refers to a person of mixed-race origin.

17. René Maran, *Un homme pareil aux autres* (Paris: Éditions Arc-en-ciel, 1947), 11.

18. Tyler Stovall, *Paris Noir: African Americans in the City of Light* (Boston: Houghton Mifflin, 1996), 33.

19. J. Nardal, "Pantins exotiques," 2.

20. See *La Dépêche africaine,* June 15, 1928, 3. The reviewer states, "This is a novel; a novel read with pleasure, and for two reasons: the author is sincere and is a negrophile" [C'est un roman; un roman lu avec plaisir, et pour deux raisons: l'auteur est sincere et il est nègrophile].

21. J. Nardal, "Pantins exotiques," 2.

22. During Morand's visit to New York, Van Vechten also threw a party in his honor after the publication of *Magie noire.* See Michel Fabre, *From Harlem to Paris: Black American Writers in France, 1840–1980* (Champaign-Urbana: University of Illinois Press, 1991), 72.

23. See, for instance, Du Bois's review of Claude McKay's *Banjo* in the July 1929 issue of the *Crisis.*

24. Carl Van Vechten, *Nigger Heaven* (New York: Knopf, 1926), 89.

25. Morand, *Black Magic,* 6, 8.

26. Carolly Erickson, *Josephine: A Life of the Empress* (New York: St. Martin's, 1999), 54.

27. J. Nardal, "Pantins exotiques," 2.

28. Morand, *Black Magic,* 148–49, 150.

29. J. Nardal, "Pantins exotiques," 2.

30. Morand, *Black Magic,* 172.

31. J. Nardal, "Pantins exotiques," 2.

3. LES SOEURS NARDAL AND THE CLAMART SALON

1. See Louis Achilles, preface to *"La Revue du monde noir"* (Paris: Jean-Michel Place, 1992), xv. This edition is a reprinted collection of the original issues.

2. Ibid., viii, xv.

3. See Shari Benstock, *Women of the Left Bank: Paris, 1900–1940* (Austin: University of Texas Press, 1986), 15. Gwendolyn Bennett was a notable exception. She was invited to tea at Stein's home during her one-year stay in Paris (see Michel Fabre's *From Harlem to Paris: Black American Writers in France, 1840–1980* [Urbana: University of Illinois Press, 1991], 123).

4. Flyer circulated by Nancy Cunard in 1931, qtd. in Hugh Ford's introduction to Nancy Cunard's *Negro: An Anthology,* edited and abridged with an introduction by Hugh Ford (New York: Continuum, 1996), xvii.

5. Madiana [Andrée Nardal], "The Beguine of the French Antilles," in

Cunard, *Negro*, 247–48. Also see Andrée Nardal, "Étude sur la Biguine Créole," *La Revue du monde noir* 2 (December 1931): 51–53.

6. In an interview published in *Challenge* in 1936, Paulette Nardal stated that Léo Sajous was the director. However, the review lists Louis-Jean Finot as "gérant-directeur" on the bottom of the section titled "Dans notre prochaine numéro" in October 1931. See Eslanda Goode Robeson's interview, "Black Paris," *Challenge* (June 1936): 11.

7. Ibid., 12. See also the first issue of *La Revue du monde noir* (October 1931), where Nardal and Shepard are listed as responsible for translations.

8. Paulette Nardal, qtd. in Achilles, preface, xiii. Her words are taken from an interview Achilles conducted with her in Martinique.

9. Paulette Nardal, "L'Éveil de la conscience de race chez les étudiants noirs," *La Revue du monde noir* 6 (April 1932): 25–31. A complete retranslation of this essay appears in the appendix.

10. The Management, "Our Aim," *La Revue du monde noir* 1 (October 1931): 2.

11. Henri Bergson, "Nos enquêtes," *La Revue du monde noir* 2 (December 1931): n.p.

12. Louis Achilles, "Nos enquêtes," *La Revue du monde noir* 3 (January 1932): 53.

13. Paulette Nardal, letter of November 17, 1963; qtd. in Jacques Louis Hymans, *Léopold Sédar Senghor: An Intellectual Biography* (Edinburgh: Edinburgh University Press, 1971), 42.

14. See the Archives d'outre mer in Aix-en-Provence (ADO), Slotfom (Service de liaison des originaires des territoires française d'outre mer) III, 81, no. 678, December 18, 1928. See also the October 15, November 15, and December 1 issues of *Les Continents* for coverage of the trial and for René Maran's editorials on Diagne and the trial.

15. Hymans, *Léopold Sédar Senghor,* 42. See also Georges Ngal, *Aimé Césaire: Un homme à la recherche d'une patrie* (Paris: Présence Africaine, 1994).

16. Senghor biographer Hymans insists that Senghor could not have developed his Negritude without Paulette Nardal and *La Revue*. See Hymans, *Léopold Sédar Senghor,* 36.

17. Léopold Senghor, "Comment nous sommes devenus ce que nous sommes," *Afrique action* 16 (January 30, 1961): 16–18.

18. P. Nardal, "Éveil," 31.

19. The Management, "Our Aim," 2.

20. H. M. Bernelot-Moens, "L'Humanité peut-elle être humanisé?" *La Revue du monde noir* 4 (February 1932): 5.

21. Janet Vaillant, *Black, French, and African: A Life of Léopold Sédar Senghor* (Cambridge: Harvard University Press, 1990), 95. Also, according to a report filed on November 9, 1928 (Slotfom III, 81, no. 595), there were tensions between blacks in the Ligue de défense de la race nègre who "flirt[ed] with

communism" and were boycotted by the "Garveyistes pan-noir." The Garveyites were supported, according to the administration's report, by the Comité de défense des interêts de la race noire and its organ, *La Dépêche africaine.*

22. Achilles, preface, xi.

23. Léo Sajous, "Les Noirs Américains au Liberia," *La Revue du monde noir* 2 (December 1931): 1–14.

24. For more on Liberia, see James Wesley Smith's *Sojourners in Search of Freedom: The Settlement of Liberia by Black Americans* (Lanham, Md.: University Press of America, 1987); Alexander Crummell's *The Future of Africa: Being Addresses, Sermons, etc., etc., Delivered in the Republic of Liberia by the Reverend Alexander Crummell* (New York: Negro Universities Press, 1969); Charles Johnson, *Bitter Canaan: The Story of the Negro Republic,* with introductory essay by John Stanfield (New Brunswick, N.J.: Transaction, 1987); and I. K. Sundiata, *Black Scandal: America and the Liberian Labor Crisis, 1929–1936* (Philadelphia: Institute for the Study of Human Issues, 1980).

25. Smith, *Sojourners in Search of Freedom,* 189–202.

26. Johnson, *Bitter Canaan,* 85.

27. Ibid., xiii.

28. Stanfield, introductory essay to *Bitter Canaan,* lix.

29. Ibid.

30. Johnson, *Bitter Canaan,* 93.

31. Sajous, "Les Noirs Américains au Liberia," 12.

32. W. E. B. Du Bois, "Negro at Paris," in *Writings by W. E. B. Du Bois in Periodicals Edited by Others,* vol. 2, *1910–1934,* ed. Herbert Aptheker (Millwood, N.Y.: Kraus-Thomson Organization, 1982), 127.

33. Nancy Cunard, "Jamaica—The Negro Island," in Cunard, *Negro,* 283.

34. Sajous, "Les Noirs Américains au Liberia," 13.

35. See Philippe Dewitte, *Les Mouvements nègres en France, 1919–1939* (Paris: L'Harmattan, 1985), 326–32. *La Race nègre* folded in February 1932, only to resurface in 1934 with a fierce black nationalism.

36. E. Grégoire-Micheli, "La Mentalité des Noirs est-elle inférieure?" *La Revue du monde noir* 2 (December 1931): 19–20.

37. See Richard J. Herrnstein and Charles Murray, *The Bell Curve: Intelligence and Class Structure in American Life* (New York: Free Press, 1994).

38. Louis-Jean Finot, "Egalité des Races," *La Revue du monde noir* 1 (October 1931): 5.

39. See E. Sicard, "Une Manifestation à l'Exposition coloniale de Vincennes," *La Revue du monde noir* 1 (October 1931): 61–62; the review of Joseph Folliet's *Le Droit de colonisation* in *La Revue du monde noir* 2 (December 1931): 54–55; and Philppe de Zara, "L'Éveil du monde noir," *La Revue du monde noir* 4 (February 1932): 1–4.

40. Finot, "Égalité des Races," 5–6.

41. Maurice Delafosse, qtd. in Grégoire-Micheli, "La Mentalité," 23–24.

42. Grégoire-Micheli, "La Mentalité," 24.
43. Clara W. Shepard, "Les Noirs Américains et les langues étrangères," *La Revue du monde noir* 4 (February 1932): 28–31.
44. Grégoire-Micheli, "La Mentalité," 25.

4. PAULETTE NARDAL

1. Paulette Nardal, "L'Éveil de la conscience de race chez les étudiants noirs," *La Revue du monde noir* 6 (April 1932): 30. See the appendix for an edited retranslation of this essay.
2. Jules Michelet, *L'Introduction à l'histoire universelle* (Paris: Librairie Armand Colin, 1962), 64.
3. Alain Locke, "The New Negro" in *The New Negro*, ed. Alain Locke (New York: Atheneum, 1969), 3–4.
4. P. Nardal, "Éveil," 26.
5. Ibid., 27.
6. Ibid.
7. Although Nardal does not mention any black women writers from the United States in this essay, she does discuss an African American woman orator's recital in Geneva and Cambridge, England, in the first issue of the review (October 1931).
8. P. Nardal, "Éveil," 27.
9. Eslanda Goode Robeson, 'Black Paris," *Challenge* (June 1936): 9.
10. P. Nardal, "Éveil," 28.
11. Étienne Léro, "Misère d'une poésie," *Légitime défense* 1 (June 1932): 10–11.
12. P. Nardal, "Éveil," 28.
13. Roberte Horth, "Histoire sans importance," *La Revue du monde noir* 2 (December 1931): 48–50.
14. Mayotte Capécia, *Je suis Martiniquaise* (Paris: Corrêa, 1948), 178, 181.
15. Horth, "Histoire sans importance," 50.
16. See Robeson, "Black Paris," 10.
17. Capécia, *Je suis Martiniquaise,* 202.
18. P. Nardal, "Éveil," 30.
19. Frantz Fanon, *Towards the African Revolution: Political Essays,* trans. Haakon Chevalier (New York: Grove, 1967), 20.
20. P. Nardal, "Éveil," 31.
21. See Janet Vaillant, *Black, French, and African: A Life of Léopold Sédar Senghor* (Cambridge: Harvard University Press, 1990), 98.

5. SUZANNE CÉSAIRE

1. Lilyan Kesteloot, *Black Writers in French: A Literary History of Negritude,* trans. Ellen Conroy Kennedy (Washington, D.C.: Howard University Press, 1991), 237.

2. René Ménil, "Généralités sur 'l'écrivain' de couleur antillais," *Légitime défense* 1 (June 1932): 8; Ménil's italics.

3. Ibid.

4. Suzanne Césaire, "Misère d'une poésie: John Antoine-Nau," *Tropiques* 4 (January 1942): 49–50.

5. Suzanne Césaire, "Malaise d'une civilisation," *Tropiques* 5 (April 1942): 48. See the appendix for the complete translated text.

6. Suzanne Césaire, "1943: Le Surréalisme et nous," *Tropiques* 8–9 (October 1943): 18.

7. Étienne Léro, René Ménil, Jules-Marcel Monnerot, Maurice-Sabas Quitman, and Simone Yoyotte, "Déclaration," *Légitime défense* 1 (June 1932).

8. Interestingly enough, *Légitime défense,* unlike *Tropiques,* did not straddle the fence between Negritude and surrealism: it is clearly surrealist in its "Déclaration" of 1932, but often it, rather than Paulette Nardal's "L'Éveil de la conscience de race chez les étudiants noirs" and *L'Étudiant noir,* is erroneously cited by scholars as the precursor to Negritude. See, for instance, Kesteloot's literary evolution in *Black Writers in French.*

9. André Breton, *Manifestoes of Surrealism,* trans. Richard Seaver and Helen Lane (Ann Arbor: University of Michigan Press, 1969), 26.

10. Originally in André Breton, *Entretiens* (Paris: Gallimard, 1969), 155–56; translation taken from *What Is Surrealism? Selected Writings of André Breton,* ed. Franklin Rosemont (London: Pluto, 1978), 256.

11. Michael Richardson, *Refusal of the Shadow: Surrealism and the Caribbean,* trans. Krzysztof Fijalkowski and Michael Richardson (London: Verso, 1996), 23.

12. Paulette Nardal, "L'Éveil de la conscience de race chez les étudiants noirs," *La Revue du monde noir* 6 (April 1932): 29. A retranslation of this essay appears in the appendix.

13. Richardson, *Refusal of the Shadow,* 7. Also see Penelope Rosemont, ed., *Surrealist Women: An International Anthology* (Austin: University of Texas Press, 1998).

14. René Ménil, "Pour une lecture critique de *Tropiques,*" in *Tropiques: Collection complète, 1941–1945* (Paris: Jean-Michel Place, 1978), xxvii, xxxi–xxxii, xxxiv.

15. "Entretien avec Aimé Césaire par Jacqueline Leiner," in *Tropiques: Collection complète,* vi.

16. Aimé Césaire, "Présentation," *Tropiques* 1 (April 1941): 5.

17. Suzanne Césaire, "Léo Frobenius et le problème des civilisations," *Tropiques* 1 (April 1941): 36.

18. René Ménil, "Naissance de notre art," *Tropiques* 1 (April 1941): 54.

19. "Lettre du Lieutenant de Vaisseau Bayle, chef du service d'information, au directeur de la revue *Tropiques,*" in *Tropiques: Collection complète,* xxxvii. See the complete translation of the letter in the appendix.

20. "Réponse de *Tropiques*," in *Tropiques: Collection complète*, xxxvix. See the complete translation in the appendix.

21. S. Césaire, "1943: Le Surrealisme et nous," 15.

22. Leo Frobenius, "Le Spiritisme dans l'intérieur de l'Afrique," *La Revue du monde noir* 5 (March 1932).

23. Léopold Senghor, "Lessons of Leo Frobenius," in *Léo Frobenius: An Anthology*, ed. Eike Haberland (Wiesbaden, Germany: Franz Steiner Verlag GMBH, 1973), vii. See also Léo Frobenius, *Histoire de la civilisation africaine*, trans. H. Back and D. Ermont (Paris: Gallimard, 1952).

24. Leo Frobenius, "On the Morphological Method of Studying Cultures" and "The Nature of Culture," in *Léo Frobenius*, 15, 20–21.

25. Frobenius, "Nature of Culture," 20.

26. S. Césaire, "Malaise d'une civilisation," 43.

27. Joseph Zobel, *La Rue Cases-Nègres: Roman* (Paris: Présence Africaine, 1984).

28. S. Césaire, "Malaise d'une civilisation," 47.

29. Suzanne Césaire, "Le Grand camouflage," *Tropiques* 13–14 (September 1945): 268. See the appendix for the complete translated text.

30. Frantz Fanon, *Black Skin, White Masks*, ed. Charles Lam Markmann (New York: Grove, 1967), 46.

31. S. Césaire, "Le Grand camouflage," 271.

32. Aimé Césaire, *Cahier d'un retour au pays natal/Return to My Native Land*, bilingual ed. (Paris: Présence Africaine Éditions, 1971), 60/61.

33. S. Césaire, "Le Grand camouflage," 273.

EXOTIC PUPPETS

1. Nardal confuses Missouri with Mississippi. *Capresse* is Antillean slang for *métisse* or *mûlatresse*.

THE AWAKENING OF RACE CONSCIOUSNESS AMONG BLACK STUDENTS

The original French title is "L'Éveil de la conscience de race chez les étudiants noirs." Nardal's English translation is: "The Awakening of Race Consciousness among Negro Students." Nardal generally translates *Noir* as "Negro" (for instance, "Antillean Negroes" from *Noirs antillais*). In reference to blacks or African Americans, Nardal uses interchangeably "Afro-Americans," and "Negro Americans." We will often translate *Noir* as "black" unless "Negro" is more appropriate, and will use "black Americans," "African Americans," and "Afro-Americans." This retranslation will attempt to stay as close to Nardal's translation of her essay as possible so as not to lose the style and voice of the author. Modifications, however, are necessary in places to clarify the meaning; it is useful to bear in mind that Nardal was more at home in French than English. It must be noted that Nardal uses the masculinist language that seemed to dominate writing of this era. Where possible, we opt for gender-neutral phrases. This is not always possible, however. Hence, the proceeding is, in effect, a "modified translation" of the 1932 English translation. All endnotes have been added to this and subsequent translations in the appendix.

1. The original is "âme nègre."

2. Friedrich Sieburg, *Dieu est-il français?* (Paris: Bernard Grasset, 1930), 76–82.

3. Here Nardal translates "finissent par se tourner vers l'élément qui leur faisait le plus honneur" as "should in the end return to the element that honored them most." But her translation does not clearly express the original French. In effect, because Antilleans were ignorant of Negro/African/Caribbean history, they would hold in esteem the element with which they were most familiar and that provided a sense of honor: the white element.

4. Unlike the United States, which maintained a "one-drop rule" with regard to the racial category of "black" and the denial of political and social rights, under French governance "métis," "mulattoes," "quadroons," and "octoroons" shared certain privileges and rights denied their darker Antillean brethren. Hence, the struggle for equality was as much an internal political and social struggle as it was a struggle against French colonial policy.

5. Lafcadio Hearn, *Two Years in the French West Indies* (published in French as *Esquisses martiniquaises*) (New York: Harper, 1890).

6. According to Michel Fabre, it was Paulette Nardal herself who wrote on Harriet Beecher Stowe. See *From Harlem to Paris: Black American Writers in France, 1840–1980* (Urbana: University of Illinois Press, 1991), 152.

LETTER FROM LIEUTENANT DE VAISSEAU BAYLE

1. Under the Vichy regime, paper was in extremely short supply in Martinique and accordingly rationed by the colonial administration. The situation, as the letter attests, made for an effective form of censorship.

2. Jean de la Fontaine, "Le Villageois et le serpent," in *Fables choisies mises en vers* (Paris, 1668); editors' translation.

3. The close of the letter is formulaic, as befits administrative protocols.

THE MALAISE OF A CIVILIZATION

Among other things, the title plays on the French translation of Sigmund Freud's *Civilization and Its Discontents* [Malaise de la civilisation].

1. Suzanne Césaire's italics, as are all others unless otherwise noted. She is here alluding to the theories of the ethnologist Leo Frobenius. See her essay "Léo Frobenius et le problème des civilisations," *Tropique* 1 (April 1941): 27–36.

THE GREAT CAMOUFLAGE

1. *Mabouyas* is Creole for a type of small lizard.

2. The allusion is to the infamous "one-drop rule" that defines racial differences as absolute in the United States alone.

3. *Mapou* is Creole for silk-cotton tree.

Selected Bibliography

SUZANNE CÉSAIRE

"Leo Frobenius et le problème des civilisations." *Tropiques* 1 (April 1941): 27–36.
"Alain et esthètique." *Tropiques* 2 (July 1941): 53–61.
"André Breton, poète." *Tropiques* 3 (October 1941): 31–37.
"Misère d'une poésie: John Antoine-Nau." *Tropiques* 4 (January 1942): 48–50.
"Malaise d'une civilisation." *Tropiques* 5 (April 1942): 43–49.
"1943: Le Surréalisme et nous." *Tropiques* 8–9 (October 1943): 14–18.
"Le Grand camouflage." *Tropiques* 13–14 (September 1945): 267–73.

Note: All of Césaire's writings listed here are also reprinted in *Tropiques: Collection complète, 1941–1945* (Paris: Jean-Michel Place, 1978).

JANE NARDAL

"Internationalisme noir." *La Dépêche africaine,* February 15, 1928, 5.
"Pantins exotiques." *La Dépêche africaine,* October 15, 1928, 2.
[Yadhé, pseud.]. "Le Soir tombe sur Karukera." *La Revue du monde noir* 4 (February 1932): 42–43.

PAULETTE NARDAL

"Le Nègre et l'art dramatique." *La Dépêche africaine,* May 15, 1928, 4.
"Le Concert du 6 octobre de la Salle Hoche." *La Dépêche africaine,* November 15, 1928, 6.
"Actions de grâces." *La Dépêche africaine,* May 30, 1929, 3.
"La Nouveau bal nègre de la glacière." *La Dépêche africaine,* May 30, 1929, 3.
"En exil." *La Dépêche africaine,* December 15, 1929, 6.
"Musique nègre: Antilles et AfraAmérique." *La Dépêche africaine,* June 30, 1930, 5.

"Une femme sculpteur noire." *La Dépêche africaine,* August–September 30, 1930, 5.

Guide des colonies: Martinique, Guadeloupe, Guyane française. Paris: Société d'éditions géographiques, maritimes et coloniales, 1931.

"Une noire parle à Cambridge et à Genève." *La Revue du monde noir* 1 (October 1931): 36–37.

"L'Éveil de la conscience de race chez les étudiants noirs." *La Revue du monde noir* 6 (April 1932): 25–31.

"Guignol ouolof." *L'Étudiant noir* 1 (March 1935): 4–5.

Index

T. Denean Sharpley-Whiting teaches French, film studies, comparative literature, and women studies, and directs the African American Studies and Research Center, at Purdue University. She is author of *Black Venus: Sexualized Savages, Primal Fears, and Primitive Narratives in French* and *Frantz Fanon: Conflicts and Feminisms.* She is coeditor of *The Black Feminist Reader*; *Spoils of War: Women of Color, Cultures, and Revolutions*; and *Fanon: A Critical Reader.*